the *first* really useful cookbook

favourite recipes from the R.D.A.

Chris Gow

Published 1994
Argyll Publishing
Glendaruel
Argyll PA22 3AE

British Library Cataloguing-in-Publication Data.
A catalogue record for this book is available from the British Library.

ISBN 1 874640 90 4

Cover design & illustrations
Marcia Clark

Printed & bound
Martins the Printers,
Berwick-upon-Tweed TD15 1RS

A really useful memorial
to my wonderful parents
Val and Ken Temple
with love.

I saw a child who couldn't walk
Sit on a horse, laugh and talk,
Then ride it through a field of daisies
And yet who could not walk unaided.
I saw a child, no legs below,
Sit on a horse and make it go
Through woods of green
And places he had never been
To sit and stare,
Except from a chair.
I saw a child who could only crawl
Mount a horse and sit up tall.
Put it through degrees of paces
And laugh at the wonder in our faces.
I saw a child born into strife,
Take up and hold the reins of life.
And that same child was heard to say,
Thank God for showing me the way.

John Anthony Davies

foreword

1994 marks the Silver Jubilee of the Association and the work it has done to provide opportunities of riding and driving for disabled people throughout the U K.

For each of us involved with the Association as members, supporters or helpers I am sure the greatest possible reward for our input is the pleasure and joy so often seen in the face of a disabled person who, unable to do so many things unaided, on a horse has independence and can, quite literally, ride tall and proud.

People of all ages and from all walks of life give of their time and money to ensure that every year more children and adults with physical or mental disadvantages can take part in therapeutic riding through which they can challenge and expand their own limitations. I suspect that many of us will never fully appreciate the sense of liberation and exhilaration so often expressed by disabled riders as they achieve yet another personal goal such as sitting unaided for the first time, or trotting. I do know, however, for many helpers have told me, that there is very real satisfaction in being able to contribute in some way to such progress.

This book of recipes is representative of so many facets of the Association – there are contributions from riders, members and supporters. Well known people from the equestrian world, from other fields of sport and from the world of entertainment have given their support to this book as they so often do to the Association. You too are now helping us and we are truly grateful for your support and your generosity.

Thank you.

Roger Bannister

Sir Roger Bannister, CBE, DM, FRCP
Honorary Life Vice-President
Riding for the Disabled Association

acknowledgements

This book owes its existence to my father, Kenneth Temple; to him a very big thank you.

But it was because of the foresight, enthusiasm, guidance and constant support of Annabelle Younger, Chairman of the Silver Jubilee Committee and formerly Chairman of West & Central Scotland Region and Ann Cooper, Publicity Officer for the region (in which I live) that it came to fruition; I owe them both a great debt.

To Anne Thorpe and all members of the Publications Committee for their positive support, comments, guidance and recipe contributions, thank you. The staff at the Headquarters of the R.D.A. with their director Dick Moss have been marvellous, always patient with my many requests and queries and happy to talk and advise me on anything I have asked or wanted. Thank you to Elizabeth Dendy, the Chairman, for her continual support and advice, and to Verona Kitson for her very useful information about the early days and people, also to Betty Kenneth for sharing her considerable experience and who has enthusiastically sent out information about the book to the groups and the public, and together with Veronica North has sold this recipe book from the R.D.A. stalls at numerous equestrian events.

Sir Roger Bannister kindly contributed the Foreword. To him and the other celebrities who sent their favourite recipes or who wrote to say they didn't have one or couldn't cook but wished the book well, my grateful thanks.

There are 18 regions and 740 RDA groups in the U.K. and it is to them, their riders, drivers, helpers and supporters that I owe a big thank you for all their time and trouble in sending me the recipes and information.

Nicky Bell helped with testing recipes and I appreciated her comments and recommendations.

To Karen MacLure who has patiently and good humouredly interpreted my writing and translated the recipes into the typed word I owe my very sincere thanks. Derek Rodger of Argyll Publishing has demonstrated his faith in this cookbook and has guided, suggested and helped progress it over the past year. To him and Marcia Clark, who designed the cover, thank you.

So many people have helped with this book in so many ways that I'm sure there must be those I haven't thanked personally so let me do that publicly, here and now.

Finally I want to thank my family and friends who have cheerfully eaten their way through the book! and given useful criticism and endless encouragement. For Iain, my husband, with his unfailing encouragement and real support in so many ways, many thank you's with my love.

Chris Gow
August 1994

introduction

First things first – I very much hope that you will get pleasure in equal measure from reading, cooking and eating these interesting recipes that have come from every part of the country and from the knowledge that every single recipe is providing financial benefit to the RDA.

Let me explain the book's title, "The First Really Useful Cookbook". When I first approached the RDA groups asking for recipes the response was tremendous. I also had lots of good wishes for the book and comments about the recipes. But by far the most common were, "If I ever had time for cooking!" or, "really useful, can be left in the oven whilst out for a day's driving/riding" and "this is a really useful recipe....."; it was such a frequently used phrase that it seemed to fall naturally into place as the book's title.

One problem was that with almost 1,000 recipes from the 18 RDA regions and only space in a modest sized book for around 200 of them a choice obviously had to be made. This was very difficult and there were contributions I just didn't want to leave out but had to so I decided to call this "The FIRST Really Useful Cookbook", and if you like it, well, you have been warned.......

I asked for traditional regional recipes where possible and I have been rewarded with an interesting collection reflecting the influence of foods available in different parts of the country. Many are family recipes, steeped in history, which have been passed down through the generations. Others have sent favourite recipes from a variety of cuisines, covering food, drink, dishes that can be made quickly, ideas for lunch and dinner parties, children's parties and of course many ideas which are useful fund raisers such as preserves, cakes and sweets.

Because the recipes have come from so many different people it was inevitable that the style and measures would vary. I have tried, I hope successfully, to bring them together in a more regular format and yet not to change them so that each retains its original individuality. Some recipes give very detailed instructions, others assume the cook knows a bit about cooking. This is first and foremost a collection of recipes and ideas. Cooking is an individual art and the final interpretation is up to you. Weights and measures were quoted in various systems. I have given both imperial and metric units using what I have judged to be a sensible approximation of one to the other. I have also tried to make the book easy to read, and you will not have to turn the page in the middle of cooking!

One of the fascinating aspects of collecting the contributions has been the immense amount of information I have received from groups about their activities, their riders/drivers, helpers and their hopes for the future. So many groups need money, not only to fund the ongoing riding sessions but to buy new ponies, purchase tack, driving carts, build arenas and many other projects. I have tried, where possible, to use some of that information in conjunction with the appropriate recipe to give a picture of the local group and thus a broader picture of the work of the RDA throughout the country.

I have thoroughly enjoyed bringing this book together. It has introduced me to so many different (and different versions of) good, honest, well tried recipes and I hope that you too enjoy using "The First Really Useful Cookbook" and that it brings you pleasure.

Christine H. Gow
Woodside Group
West & Central Scotland Region

Riding for the Disabled Association

HRH The Princess Royal President, visiting Winton group and presenting "Sweetie" the RDA pony, aged 31, with a Long Service Award.

Getting to know you.

Everyone can lend a hand.

a brief history

The Riding for the Disabled Association was inspired by the example set by Liz Hartel, a disabled Danish rider, in winning a silver medal at the Helsinki Olympic Games in 1952.

During the 1950s and early 60s, the possibilities of introducing riding as an activity to benefit and to be enjoyed by disabled people were explored. Several pioneers came together in 1964 and formed 8 groups.

Five years later, in 1969, the Riding for the Disabled Association was formed. By then the enterprise had grown into 80 groups and a total of 2,400 riders.

Now, in its Silver Jubilee Year, the RDA has more than 700 member groups throughout the UK, (and over 20 associated overseas groups worldwide) and provides the opportunity for both riding and driving to well over 25,000 adults and children, made possible by 15,000 voluntary helpers.

an opportunity for all

Each member group is different, varying greatly in size and location, and in the facilities and opportunities they offer.

There are now 22 purpose-built or adapted centres throughout the British Isles, each owning their own horses and ponies, and catering for several hundred riders.

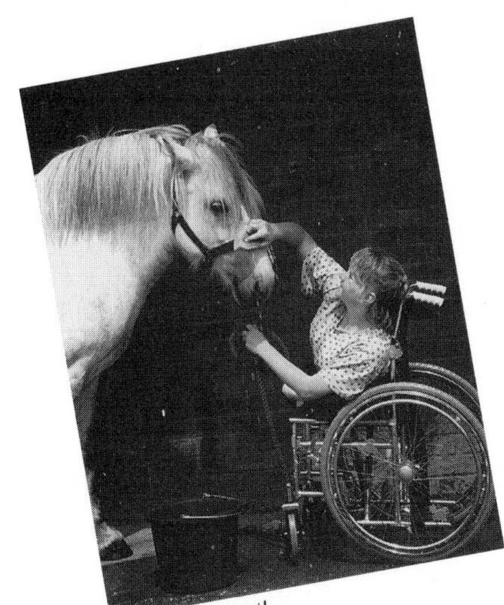
Shampoo and set!

Poise and elegance.

But just as important, are the hundreds of local riding schools which offer their facilities every week.

Indeed, there's a wealth of opportunity for all to take part – not only the riders themselves, but also the legions of warm-hearted volunteers who give so freely of their time and effort.

fun on four legs!

Large or small, town or country-based, each group works wholeheartedly to achieve the RDA's mission – "To provide the opportunity for riding and driving to disabled people who might benefit in their general health and well being".

In this landmark year, the RDA is seeking to widen the support it already enjoys and so realise ambitious plans. It aims to –

* Create more facilities – particularly in urban areas

* Attract more voluntary helpers

* Broaden training activities for helpers and instructors

* Fund research into medical benefits of riding for disabled people

* Help riders and drivers to achieve their personal goals

Volunteers are needed to help in most groups. You don't need to be 'horsey', there are plenty of jobs to be done!

And you can also help by making a donation to help pay for specialist equipment, the hire and care of ponies, contributions to riding holidays and a host of other needs.

Going along nicely.

a driving ambition!

Driving was introduced to the RDA in 1974 to give physically disabled adults, who were unable to ride, the opportunity to enjoy the benefits of a sport and animal related activity.

Drivers, many of whom are confined to a wheelchair, can enjoy the countryside and the company of able-bodied whips and the horse in open vehicles specially designed to meet their particular needs.

A picnic break for all.

getting away!

Riders and drivers can be any age from mere toddlers to octogenarians! Many disabilities are greatly helped by the movement of the horse, which in turn helps to strengthen back muscles and improve head control.

But, in many instances, it's the feeling of companionship, of being involved in exercises and games, that produces a beneficial therapeutic effect.

Riding and driving holidays are very popular, providing new experiences, widening horizons, increasing confidence, and developing a real sense of independence.

It's great to be in the saddle!

"thank you"

The needs of the disabled rider and driver are ever-pressing. We need more voluntary helpers and we need more funds.

Whilst each Group is supported by its own fund-raising efforts and donations, there is always a need to give support at national level, particularly in providing more purpose-built and self-managed RDA centres.

Please help us to help others to learn a new skill, and to bring more fun and enjoyment into their lives.

I love my pony!

If you would like to know more about the work of the Riding for the Disabled Association or feel that you could support and help a Group in any way RDA's National Headquarters will be pleased to hear from you. For further information about your local Group(s) just contact –

The Riding for the Disabled Association

National Headquarters
Avenue 'R'
National Agricultural Centre
Kenilworth CV8 2LY
Tel: 0203-696510
Fax: 0203-696532

contents

Wine recommendations throughout
are courtesy of Safeway.

soups & starters

Eat Your Oats Up - Easy Onion Soup

This is cold weather soup – quick to make with ingredients that are usually in the cupboard.

(Serves 4-6 people).

1oz (25g)	butter
8oz (225g)	onion, finely chopped
1oz (25g)	medium oatmeal
1pt (570ml)	chicken stock
1/2 pt (275ml)	milk
1/4 pt (150ml)	cream (optional)
Salt and freshly ground black pepper	

In a large heavy based saucepan melt the butter and add the chopped onion, fry gently until cooked. Add the oatmeal and cook for 1 minute. Remove the pan from the heat and gradually add the chicken stock, stirring all the time to prevent the oatmeal from going lumpy. Return to the heat and cook gently for about 1/2 an hour. Add the milk just before serving, reheat but do not allow to boil. Season to taste. If special add the 1/4 pint of cream.

M. QUARM, WINTON GROUP, WEST & CENTRAL SCOTLAND REGION

Started 21 years ago with one class. Today there are seven classes over four days giving lessons to 48 riders, children and young adults from local special schools and adult training centres who live locally in Irvine, Kilwinning, Beith and Dalry.

Quick Tomato Soup

This really is quick – the cooking time is 10 – 15 minutes. Useful for busy riders.

(Serves 4-6 people)

1	onion, any size, finely chopped
2 cloves	garlic (optional) chopped
2 tblsp	olive oil
1/2 tsp	dried marjoram
1/2 tsp	thyme
14oz (400g)	can peeled tomatoes + 1 can water
14oz (400g)	can baked beans + 1 can water
1/2 tsp	sugar
Salt and freshly ground black pepper	

Gently cook the onion and garlic in the olive oil, add the dried herbs and when softened add the contents of the cans and the water. Process all, or half, depending on your preference. Add sugar, salt and pepper to taste.

NICKY STARKS, PUBLICATIONS COMMITTEE

Artichoke and Carrot Soup

Artichokes impart a very delicate and distinctive flavour. They also blend well with mushrooms to produce a "white" soup.

(Serves 6-8 people)

$1^1/_2$ lb (700g)	Jerusalem Artichokes
1 dsp	lemon juice
1lb (450g)	carrots, chopped
2oz (50g)	butter
4oz (110g)	onion chopped
4oz (110g)	celery, chopped
$2^1/_2$ pt (1.5ltrs)	chicken stock
$^1/_4$ pt (150ml)	cream (optional)
Salt and freshly ground black pepper	

Prepare the artichokes by removing the knobs, and peeling. Roughly slice/ chop and if you are not ready to use immediately keep in a bowl of water with a dessertspoonful of lemon juice added. This prevents discolouration.

Melt the butter in a saucepan and cook the celery and onion for a few minutes. Add the artichokes (well drained if you have had them in water) and carrots, toss them in the butter, replace the lid and cook for about 5 minutes. Stir in the stock, and simmer for about 20 minutes, until the vegetables are tender. Remove from the heat and allow to cool before liquidizing, passing through the sieve or mouli until it is very smooth. Cream may be added at this point if you wish. Reheat (but do not boil if you added cream). Adjust seasoning and serve.

JENNY WILLS, EAST LODGE FARM GROUP, MOULTON, NORTH MIDLANDS REGION

Summer Soup

(Serves 4-6 people)

$^1/_2$ pt (275ml)	tomato juice
$^1/_2$ pt (275ml)	chicken stock
$^1/_2$ pt (275ml)	orange juice
3 floz (75ml)	sherry
1 tblsp	lemon juice (strained)
1 tsp	sugar
Salt and freshly ground black pepper	
3floz (75ml)	cream (optional)
1 tblsp	chopped mint

Mix the tomato juice, stock, orange juice, sherry, lemon juice and sugar together, heat gently until the sugar is dissolved, about 5 minutes. Add cream if you wish, adjust the seasoning. Serve hot or very cold with a blob of cream and a sprinkling of chopped mint.

CRANLEIGH GROUP, SOUTH EAST REGION

Wellview's Spicy Lentil Soup

A good filling soup for cold days.
This soup freezes well.

(Serves 4-6 people)

1oz (25g)	butter
6oz (175g)	smoked streaky bacon, rinds removed and roughly chopped
4oz (125g)	onion finely chopped
1 clove	garlic finely chopped
1½ tblsp	medium curry powder
8oz (225g)	red lentils (washed & drained)
1lb (450g)	fresh tomatoes, peeled, de-seeded and roughly chopped OR
14oz (400g)	can of tomatoes
2 tblsp	tomato puree
3pts (1.75ltrs)	good chicken stock
Salt and freshly ground black pepper	
1 tblsp	freshly chopped parsley and
2 tblsp	croutons to serve with it

Melt the butter and gently fry the bacon for about 2 minutes. Add the chopped onion and garlic and cook until soft, stir in the curry powder and continue to cook gently for a minute. Add the lentils, tomatoes and tomato puree and cook for a further 2-3 minutes. Then add the stock, bring to the boil and allow to simmer gently for 45-60 minutes. Leave to cool a little before liquidizing, processing or putting through the mouli whatever is your favourite method. Reheat, adjust seasoning, and serve garnished with finely chopped parsley and/or croutons if you wish.

Note – I prefer to soak red lentils overnight, this makes them softer when cooking, and thus they need less cooking time. If you use green/brown lentils they do not need soaking.

NITHSDALE RIDING & DRIVING GROUP, EDINBURGH & BORDERS REGION

Bortsch – Beetroot Soup

This is a substantial soup – or main course soup. I found that by adding extra water it was more soupy or with the quantity in the recipe it was more of a stew. Excellent either way. Good served with crusty bread.

(Serves 6-8 people).

1lb (450g)	**meat, cubed (e.g. stewing steak)**
2 large	**potatoes**
1/2 small	**white cabbage**
2	**onions**
2	**carrots**
1 medium	**beetroot (fresh/raw)**
1/2 oz (10g)	**butter**
2	**bay leaves**
1 tblsp	**tomato puree**
Salt and freshly ground black pepper	
Small pot of sour cream or natural yogurt	

Choose a large heavy bottomed pan. Place the cubed meat in it and cover with water. Bring to the boil and then reduce the heat and allow to simmer. Meanwhile peel and cube the potatoes, add to the meat. Shred the cabbage, add to the meat. Grate the onions, carrots and beetroot and fry gently in the butter for a few minutes, add this to the "pot" when it is boiling. Add the bay leaves, and tomato puree. Simmer for about 1 1/2 hours or until the meat is tender. Skim of any excess fat. Adjust the seasoning and serve with soured cream or natural yogurt.

Janet Copley says "this recipe was given to me by Gatya, a Russian maid working for an English family resident in Moscow. She adapted the recipe according to whatever was available in the shops and would not give specific cooking times, "until it was done" was her maxim."

JANET COPLEY, WAKEFIELD LODGE GROUP, SOUTH REGION

Two schools participate – Brookfields Special School whose students are 16-19 years old and have various disabilities, and St. Michael's School, visually impaired unit, whose riders are from 5-11 years old, their sight ranges from poor to blind.

Parsnip and Cheese Soup

A delicious simple soup.

(Serves 4-6 people).

1lb (450g)	parsnips
1oz (25g)	butter
8oz (225g)	onion, finely chopped
2pts (1ltr)	stock (whichever you prefer)
	bouquet garni
2oz (50g)	cream cheese
1	orange (grated rind)
Salt and freshly ground black pepper	

Clean the parsnips, remove any woody centres and then chop fairly small. Melt the butter in a saucepan, stir in the onions and parsnips, cover and leave to cook gently for about 10 minutes. Add the stock, stirring gently.Add the bouquet garni. Bring to the boil, then reduce heat and simmer for 20 minutes. Remove the bouquet garni, and allow the soup to cool a little before liquidizing until it is smooth. Put the cheese into a saucepan and cream it gradually working in the soup. Finally stir in the orange rind and gently reheat the soup, without boiling. Adjust the seasoning.

MARY MACDONELL, HIGHLAND GROUP, GRAMPIAN & HIGHLAND REGION

Founded in 1975 and now has over 285 riders and drivers with a wide range of physical and mental handicaps and some riders who are deaf, dumb or blind. Happily they have been able to help rehabilitate people after accidents and illnesses.

Summer Fish Soup

Serve chilled.

(Serves 4 – 6 people)

14oz (400g)	can Lobster Bisque
3/4 (425ml)	tomato juice
1/2	lemon, the juice
1/4 pt (150ml)	single cream
pinch of	cayenne pepper
4oz (110g)	shelled shrimps, roughly chopped
salt and freshly ground black pepper	
To finish	
4-6 tblsp	single cream
2 tblsp	chopped parsley

Put bisque, tomato and lemon juice, cream and cayenne pepper in a bowl and beat well. Stir in the shrimps, salt and pepper. Stir thoroughly and serve with a swirl of cream and a sprinkle of parsley.

Can be frozen before adding final cream.

KATHLEEN HODGSON, THE DIAMOND RIDING GROUP, GREATER LONDON REGION

The Diamond Centre has both riding and driving facilities.

From Martin Pipe

Melon Eden

This is a favourite recipe of mine – delicious. It makes a summer lunch main course for one person, or alternatively cut the melon into halves, thus making two starters.

1	Ogen melon
2½ oz (60g)	prawns
2½ oz (60g)	smoked salmon
2 dsp	marie rose sauce

Cut the ogen top off about a quarter of the way down.

Take out all the seeds. Scoop out the melon into small balls. Slice the smoked salmon into thin strips and mix with the prawns, melon balls and marie rose sauce.

Put the mixture back into the melon, drape a few prawns over the side of the melon.

Tip – cut a thin slice off the bottom of the melon so that it will stand up.

MARTIN PIPE

The most successful National Hunt trainer in history. His record includes 6 years as "most winners in the season" and his partnership with jockey Peter Scudamore has established levels of success that will be hard to match.

Smoked Salmon with a difference

(Serves 4 – 6 people)

1	avocado pear
2 tblsp	lemon juice
½	honeydew melon
6oz (175g)	smoked salmon, thinly sliced
¼ pt (150ml)	double cream
2 tblsp	mayonnaise
1 tblsp	tomato ketchup
salt and freshly ground black pepper	
slices of lemon for garnish	

Peel and slice the avocado and toss in lemon juice to prevent discolouration. Peel and slice the melon – paring it to the same size as the avocado. Wrap a slice of each with the smoked salmon.

Place the rolls, join side down on a small plate.

Lightly whip the double cream, fold in the mayonnaise and tomato ketchup. Season to taste. Then spoon the sauce over the smoked salmon rolls, and serve with a slice of avocado, melon and lemon.

AVONDALE AND DISTRICT GROUP, WEST AND CENTRAL SCOTLAND REGION

From Miss T. Martin Bird

Prawns with Cream and Brandy Sauce

(Serves 4 people)

1 1/2 oz (40g)	butter
8oz (225g)	prawns
1/4 pt (150ml)	cream
small glass of brandy	
seasoning	freshly ground black pepper
	lemon juice
	nutmeg
	parsley, finely chopped
2oz (50g)	patna rice, cooked

Heat the butter in a frying pan and gently sauté the well seasoned prawns for about 2 minutes.Heat the brandy, and pour flaming over the prawns, shaking the pan so that the flames spread. When the flames are out turn the heat to low and continue to cook for a further minute or two to reduce the liquid.

Turn up the heat, add the cream and allow it to bubble until it starts to thicken. Shake the pan and spoon the cream up and round the prawns.

Stir in a little finely chopped parsley and serve the prawns on top of the rice.

MISS TESSA MARTIN BIRD

Vice-President RDA. Fellow of the British Horse Society and the trainer on television of the Blue Peter pony, Rags for the use of the RDA.

East Neuk Shrimp

(Serves 4 people)

4oz (110g)	shelled shrimps or prawns
1/2 pt (275ml)	cream
4 tblsp	white breadcrumbs
salt and freshly ground black pepper	
3oz (75g)	butter

Pre-heat oven to 350°F, 180°C, Gas 4

Butter 4 ramekins, share the shrimps or prawns between them, cover with cream. Sprinkle the breadcrumbs on top, season and place a large knob of butter on each.

Place in a bain marie and bake for 10-15 minutes, until lightly browned.

JULIET OSWALD, FLICKSMILLAN DRIVING GROUP,
EDINBURGH AND BORDERS REGION

Formed in 1989 with two drivers. They now have seven drivers, two ponies, three physios, two vets and several helpers on the team. The group also organises the annual Scottish National Disabled Driving Event at St Fort.

Smoked Mussels

(Serves 4 – 6 people)

8oz (225g)	**smoked mussels**
1 clove	**garlic, crushed**
2oz (50g)	**smoked back bacon, chopped**
salt and freshly ground black pepper	

Fry the chopped bacon and garlic together. Add the mussels at the last minute just to warm through. Season.

Then either put them on an interesting salad with a little vinaigrette or add some cream and make a pasta sauce.

INGFIELD MANOR GROUP, SOUTH EAST REGION

This is a long established group which offers riding to the children of Ingfield Manor School which is a spastic society school for cerebral palsy. They meet once a week during term time and rely on their volunteers to help and bring the ponies.

Potters Paté

(Serves 6 – 8 people)

$^1/_2$ oz (10g)	**lard**
8oz (225g)	**streaky bacon, rindless**
8oz (225g)	**sausage meat**
8oz (225g)	**chicken livers**
1 large	**onion**
1 clove	**garlic**
salt and freshly ground black pepper	

Pre-heat oven to 325°F, 170°C, Gas 3

Grease a 1lb (450g) loaf tin with lard, and then line the bottom and sides with the streaky bacon.

Mince or process together the sausage meat, liver, onion and garlic. Season.

Put the mixture into the loaf tin, pressing it in firmly. Cover the top with any remaining bacon. Then a piece of parchment paper topped with foil, firmly secured round the edges. Place in a bain marie and bake for $1^1/_2$ hours.

When cooked pour off any excess fat. Make sure the top is well covered and weighted down. Refrigerate for 12 hours before turning out and slicing.

NORTH EAST DERBYSHIRE GROUP, NORTH MIDLANDS REGION

Smoked Mackerel Paté

From Ian Stark

2 fillets	smoked mackerel
knob of	butter
	lemon juice to taste
	salt and pepper to taste
1 large tub	natural yoghurt

Flake the fish fillets off the skin being careful to remove any bones. Place all the ingredients in a food processor and mix well.

Taste and adjust the seasoning. Turn into a mould or individual dishes.

This paté freezes well, and is best after it has frozen.

IAN STARK

One of Scotland's most outstanding equestrian competitors, Ian Stark's career so far has been highlighted by his participation in 3 consecutive Olympic Games (winning 2 Silver Medals) and winning the European Championship in 1991.

Grouse Paté

From Mrs C Allan

(Makes enough for 12 people)

2	old grouse, including liver & hearts (very important)
4oz (110g)	pigs liver
8oz (225g)	butter
1 small	onion
1/2	lemon, the juice
glass of	red wine
freshly ground black pepper	

Fry the grouse, livers and hearts, and the pigs liver and onions in some of the butter. Put all the meat into a stewpan, cover with water, add the lemon juice. Cover and cook until all the meat leaves the bones.

Put the meat through the fine mincer twice. The bones go back into the water in the pan. Add the wine and boil to reduce by two thirds.

Put the minced meat and remaining butter into a bowl, add the reduced liquid and beat well until creamy, mix in the black pepper to taste.

Spoon into a mould or individual dishes and refrigerate.

MRS C ALLAN

Honorary Life Vice-President of RDA. Founder of the Borders group in 1967 (one of the earliest groups), member of RDA Council and Regional representative of Edinburgh and the Borders 1971-80.

First Course Mousse

(Serves 4 people)

5	hard boiled eggs
1/2 pt (275g)	double cream
1 tbslp	Worcester sauce
1 tblsp	anchovy essence
1 pkt	aspic jelly
3/4 pt (425g)	hot water
salt and freshly ground black pepper	

Shell and chop the eggs. Whip the cream and add the Worcester Sauce, anchovy essence and eggs. Fold until well mixed.

Dissolve the aspic in the hot water and allow to cool slightly. Then add half of it, very slowly to the egg mixture continuing to fold it in.

Spoon the mousse into a souffle dish or individual ramekins. Spoon the reserved aspic on top to give a clear glaze.

Refrigerate.

HOLTWOOD GROUP, SOUTH WEST REGION

Gazpacho Mousse

(Serves 6 – 8 people)

14oz (400g)	tomato soup
8oz (275g)	cream cheese
1 pkt (10g)	gelatine
2 tblsp	water
4oz (110g)	onion, finely chopped
4oz (110g)	green pepper, finely chopped
2oz (50g)	celery, finely chopped
2oz (50g)	cucumber, peeled & finely chopped
2 tblsp	mayonnaise
8oz (225g)	peeled prawns
salt and freshly ground black pepper	

Bring the soup to the boil, melt in the cheese.

Dissolve the gelatine in the water and add to the soup – do not allow to boil – beat well and leave to cool.

Then add all the other ingredients and mix well. Taste, adjust the seasoning and spoon the mousse into individual ramekins. Refrigerate until set.

ANNE HALLEY, HEATHFIELD GROUP, SOUTH REGION

Cheese and Garlic Paté

From Lord Rix

2oz (50g)	cheese (your preference)
1oz (25g)	fresh breadcrumbs
	garlic, to taste
	mixed herbs, to taste
	mayonnaise, to taste
1/2 oz (10g)	butter, melted & cooled

Place the cheese, garlic and herbs in a blender and process for three seconds. (Alternatively, grate or use liquidizer).

Place the mixture in a bowl and fold in the breadcrumbs. Add all the melted butter and continue to add mayonnaise until the mixture achieves the consistency you require.

Place the mixture in a terrine or loaf tin and press down well and refrigerate.

THE LORD RIX, CBE, DL

Vice-President RDA. An outstanding personality in the world of theatrical farce and now as Peer of the Realm and Chairman of Mencap, an outstanding supporter and activist for those with learning disabilities.

Devilled Kidneys

Serve as a starter for hungry people or as a supper dish.

(Serves 4 people)

8	lambs kidneys
2oz (50g)	butter
8 tblsp	tomato ketchup
4 tsp	Worcester Sauce
4	thick pieces of toast
salt and freshly ground black pepper	

Prepare the kidneys (skin, cut in half and remove as much as possible of the tubes).

Cook the kidneys in melted butter for a few minutes on each side. Then place 4 halves into each of two soup pots.

In the pan add the tomato ketchup to the pan juices, the Worcester Sauce, and mix well. Bring to the boil, adjust seasoning to taste.

Pour the sauce over the kidneys in each pot and serve with slices of thick toast. When eating, the kidneys should be poured out of the pot on top of the toast.

SUKI PEAKE, ORGANISER OF THE KNIGHTSBRIDGE GROUP, GREATER LONDON REGION

Baked Cheese Log
with Basil and Pine Nuts

This is an unusual starter, ideal for serving before a light main course.

(Serves 4 people)

2 cloves	**garlic**
pinch of	**salt**
about 20	**fresh basil leaves**
1oz (25g)	**pine nuts, toasted**
3 tblsp	**olive oil**
2 tblsp	**parmesan cheese, grated**
6oz (175g)	**goat's cheese**
4 pieces of	**filo pastry 8" x 6" (20cm x 15cm)**
2oz (50g)	**butter, melted**

Pre-heat oven to 400°F, 200°C, Gas 6

Thinly slice the garlic and pound with the salt in a mortar and pestle. Tear the basil leaves into small pieces and work into the garlic and salt. Add the pine nuts and the olive oil and pound or place in a processor until sauce is smooth. Stir in the parmesan cheese.

Cut the goat's cheese into 4 slices, removing rind. Lay one piece on each sheet of pastry and spoon a tablespoon of the basil sauce over each. Brush the edges of the pastry with melted butter and wrap the pastry around the cheese to form a parcel. Brush with melted butter and place on a baking sheet. Bake for 10-15 minutes. Serve hot garnished with watercress, curly endive or lollo rosso.

IRENE HOLMES, ELIZABETH CURTIS CENTRE, EAST REGION

Cheddar Cheese Eggs

(Serves 4 people)

1oz (25g)	**butter**
3oz (75g)	**cheddar cheese, grated**
4	**eggs**
salt and freshly ground black pepper	

Pre-heat oven to 350°F, 180°C, Gas 4

Grease 4 ramekins with the butter. Put a layer of grated cheese into each ramekin. Break an egg into each. Keeping them whole. Then add another layer of cheese. Season. Place in a bain marie and bake until the eggs are set.

This is good in a microwave if you are only doing one or two.

BIDDY COCKBURN, CHARD DISTRICT GROUP, SOUTH WEST REGION

The group has grown and now has five rides of small children, teenagers and adults, together with a large and faithful band of helpers.

Twice Baked Goat Cheese and Garlic Souffle

(Serves 6 – 8 people)

For the white sauce

1½ oz (40g)	butter
1½ oz (40g)	flour
½ pt (275ml)	milk

For the rest

12oz (350g)	goats cheese (dry, crumbly type is best)
5	egg yolks
6	fat bulbs garlic
4 tblsp	white wine
4 tblsp	oil
6	egg whites
salt and freshly ground black pepper	
2oz (50g)	parmesan, freshly grated
2oz (50g)	gruyere, freshly grated
¼ pt (150ml)	double cream

Pre-heat oven to 350°F, 180°C, Gas 4

Make the white sauce, crumble the goats cheese into the sauce and simmer. Allow to cool slightly and then add the egg yolks, cook very gently (do not allow to boil) until thick. Pass through a tammy cloth, seive or whizz in the processor and cover with cling film.

Meanwhile bake the garlic with the oil and wine for 30 minutes, peel and puree. There should be 4 tablespoons of garlic puree.

Fold the garlic puree into the sauce mix. Whisk the egg whites until just stiff, fold into the sauce mixture. Adjust seasoning. Spoon mixture into individual moulds which have been well greased (or one large mould). Bake in a bain marie in the oven for 20-25 minutes until firm. Remove. Turn oven up to 400°F, 200°C, Gas 6.

Then cover each souffle with cream, topped with a little parmesan and gruyere and bake again for 10-15 minutes until golden brown. Serve immediately.

MAGGIE MACKENZIE, who drives with RUTHVEN DRIVING GROUP AT GLENEAGLES, WEST AND CENTRAL SCOTLAND REGION

Started in 1989 they meet every week, with helpers helping alternate weeks. The group owns one pony Muffin, looked after by Gleneagles Equestrian Centre and they hire Miley but he has arthritis so his contribution is limited. Presently the group is fund raising in order to purchase another driving pony.

Loch Lomond Baskets

(Serves 4 people)

1/2 lb (4) (225g)	Scottish tomatoes
3oz (75g)	low fat cottage cheese
2 tblsp	double cream
1oz (25g)	smoked ham, finely chopped
3oz (75g)	cucumber, peeled & finely chopped
1 tblsp	chives, finely chopped
salt and freshly ground black pepper	
lettuce and cucumber garnish	

Using the vandyke method (zig zagging), cut the tops off the tomatoes, or just cut straight across. Reserve the tops. Scoop out the seeds and flesh (keep for soup). Then turn the tomatoes upside down on absorbant paper.

Beat together the cottage cheese and cream, until smooth. Stir in the ham, cucumber and chives. Season.

Pipe or spoon the mixture into the tomato shells and replace the "lids". To serve, arrange the baskets on lettuce and garnish with cucumber.

FINTRY DRIVING GROUP, WEST & CENTRAL SCOTLAND REGION

Cheese Balls

(Serves 4 – 6 people)

8oz (225g)	Feta cheese
3oz (75g)	butter
small stick	celery, finely chopped
pinch of	cayenne
salt and freshly ground black pepper	
1/2 bunch	watercress, finely chopped
6oz (175g)	wholemeal breadcrumbs
1oz (25g)	parmesan cheese
1 tblsp	fresh parsley, finely chopped

Beat the Feta cheese and butter to a smooth paste, blend in the celery, seasonings and watercress.

Roll into balls and coat with a mixture of breadcrumbs, parmesan and parsley.

Chill.

MARGARET MOORE, HEREFORD GROUP, WEST MERCIA REGION

Originally started in 1969 as a Red Cross Group and funded by them, the group is now in a purpose built centre where they meet every week. They have 60 riders.

Chive Crepes
with Mushroom Filling

Serve as a starter or a light meal.

(Serves 4 – 8 people)

For the filling

1lb (450g)	button mushrooms
1oz (25g)	butter
1/2 pt (275ml)	milk
salt and freshly ground black pepper	
1/4 tsp	nutmeg
1 1/2 tblsp	lemon juice
1/2 pt (275ml)	cheese or tomato sauce

For the crepes

5oz (150g)	plain flour
1/4 tsp	salt
2	eggs
2 tblsp	chives, chopped
1 tblsp	oil

For the filling, wipe and chop the mushrooms. Heat the butter in a saucepan and fry the mushrooms for 3 minutes stirring constantly. Add milk, seasoning, nutmeg and lemon juice. Bring to the boil and simmer for 10 minutes uncovered. Strain the mixture reserving the liquid for the crepes.

To make the crepes, sift the flour and salt into a mixing bowl. Make a well in the centre and add the eggs, drawing in the flour. Mix in the chopped chives. Whisk gradually adding the reserved liquid to make a smooth batter.

Brush a little oil over the frying pan and pre-heat it. Pour in enough batter to just coat the base of the pan evenly. Cook over a high heat until the underside is golden then turn and cook for a further 1-2 minutes.

Tip onto a sheet of greaseproof paper. Repeat until all the batter is used up. Divide the filling between the pancakes and roll them to enclose the filling.

Pre-heat oven to 350°F, 180°C, Gas 4

Make a cheese or tomato sauce, arrange crepes in a greased ovenproof dish and pour the sauce over.

Bake uncovered for 20 minutes.

Serve one or two crepes as a starter or more for a main course.

BERYL BEARD, HELPER, UPMINSTER GROUP, EAST REGION

Formed in 1973 the group started with five children riding for one hour once a week. Today 35 children ride on two mornings a week, they come from various special schools in Essex. The 35 helpers who come along each week give freely of their time. There are various fund-raising activities throughout the year to help finance the group.

fish

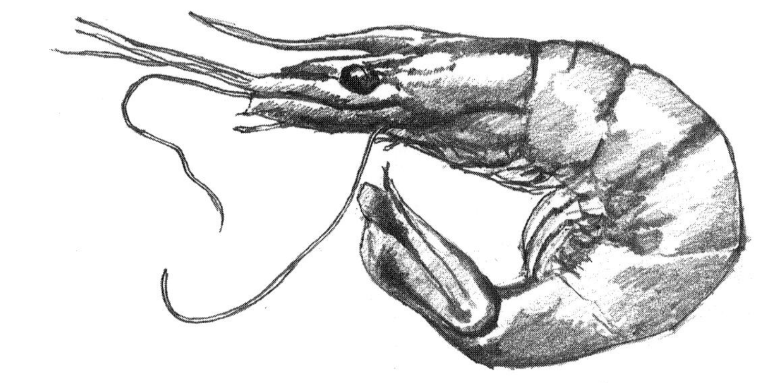

Salmon with Light Orange Sauce

(Serves 4 people)

4 x 6oz (175g) salmon steaks	
6 tblsp	white wine
a little	water
1oz (25g)	butter
1oz (25g)	flour
1/4 pt (125ml)	milk
1	orange, juice and zest
2	egg whites, beaten until stiff
salt and freshly ground black pepper	

Poach the salmon steaks in the wine and water.

Put the butter, flour, milk, orange juice, seasoning and zest of orange into a saucepan. Cook over a low heat stirring continuously until thickened and smooth. Fold in the egg whites and serve immediately with the salmon.

BARBARA WILLIS, DIGSWELL PLACE GROUP, EAST REGION

Salmon Mousse

This makes a very attractive dish for the buffet table.

(Serves 4 people)

7oz (200g) tin red salmon	
1/4 pt (150ml)	mayonnaise
1/4 pt (150ml)	double cream
1/2 oz (10g)	gelatine
2 tblsp	water
salt and freshly ground black pepper	
watercress	

Drain and flake the salmon, removing any bones. Place in a bowl and add the mayonnaise. Whisk the cream until it is the same consistency as the mayonnaise. Add to the salmon mixture.

Dissolve the gelatine in the warmed water. Add to the mixture and fold it all carefully and lightly until well blended. Adjust the seasoning and spoon into a lightly oiled mould. Refrigerate until set. Turn out and garnish with watercress.

For an economy version, use tuna for salmon and a small tin of evap milk for the cream. Add a few drops of cochineal and no one can tell the difference!

NORTH EAST DERBYSHIRE GROUP, NORTH MIDLANDS REGION

The group formed in 1979, meet 3 days a week and use the local riding school with their indoor arena, which is very necessary in the winter. They have 5 ponies, 100 riders children and adults, and helpers. The group has achieved 2 silver and a bronze medal in the musical ride competitions. A pony camp is held each year for the children when they spend one or two days under canvas and help care for the ponies. An annual sponsored ride raises some funds.

Scottish Wild Salmon

with a crust of grilled red pepper

Farmed salmon can be substituted for wild salmon.

(Serves 4 people)

4 x (6oz -175g)	**fillet of salmon**
2	**very red red peppers**
¼ tsp	**paprika, mild**
½ oz (10g)	**unsalted butter, softened**
salt and freshly ground black pepper	
¼ pt (150ml)	**medium dry white wine**

Use a pan/container that can be used on the hob, under the grill and in the oven!

Remove the skin from the salmon and check for any small bones. Sprinkle with a little salt on all sides and place in a well buttered pan; the side that had the skin on down. Chill until needed.

Cut the peppers in half, and clean. Place under a hot grill until blackened and beginning to soften. Remove the charred skin under running cold water. Dry thoroughly on kitchen paper. Then cut up and place in food processor with paprika, a little salt and freshly ground black pepper. Process, leaving some texture. Remove just over half the mixture and place in a small saucepan.

Add the butter to the remaining pepper in the processor and process briefly to mix in. Adjust seasoning. Use this mixture to spread evenly on top of the salmon steaks. Return to refrigerator until needed.

Add the white wine to the red pepper mixture in the saucepan, simmer until really softened and slightly reduced. Liquidize until smooth. Taste and if too sharp add a little sugar and single cream. Refrigerate until needed.

Remove salmon from refrigerator – allow to come to room temperature. Sauté (in a little extra butter if needed) for 2-3 minutes. Grill the top for 1-2 minutes under a very hot grill. Keep warm in the oven.

Meanwhile reheat the sauce gently. Place a little sauce on each plate. Place the salmon fillet half on the sauce and serve with a plain steamed green vegetable, e.g. broccoli and new boiled potatoes tossed in dill.

MARY HENDRY, KETTERING AND DISTRICT GROUP, NORTH MIDLANDS REGION

Salmon Steaks
with Avocado Sauce

(Serves 6 people)

6 x 6oz (175g) salmon steaks	
sprigs of tarragon or 1 tsp dried tarragon	
2	bay leaves
salt and freshly ground black pepper	
6 dsp	white wine
For the sauce	
1 large	avocado
1 clove	garlic, peeled and chopped
1 tsp	sherry vinegar
salt and freshly ground black pepper	
1 tub	creme fraiche

Pre-heat oven to 350°F, 180°C, Gas 4

Take a large sheet of foil and lay it in a shallow baking tin.

Wipe the salmon and place each steak on the foil. Place tarragon and a piece of bay leaf on each. Season with salt and freshly ground black pepper, and a dessertspoon of wine over each steak.

Wrap loosely in foil making a pleat in the top and cook in the oven for 20 minutes.

Remove from the oven and allow the salmon to "set" without opening the foil parcel until you are ready to serve it.

To make the sauce – whilst the salmon is cooking – scoop out the flesh of the avocado, making sure you scrape the green just under the skin. Place in the processor with the sherry vinegar (this helps preserve the colour). Add the garlic and seasoning and whizz.

Put the puree in a bowl and fold in the creme fraiche until well blended.

Taste to see if more sherry vinegar is needed.

Cover with cling film – excluding as much air as possible to prevent the sauce discolouring – and refrigerate.

To serve – remove the skin from each steak and hand round the sauce separately

ODETTE HARRISON, LEOMINSTER GROUP, WEST MERCIA REGION.

Strule Trout in Almonds

(Serves 2 people)

2 x 10oz (275g)	**Strule trout (freshly caught, cleaned but whole)**
$1\,^1/_2$ oz (275g)	**butter**
1 tblsp	**lemon juice**
2	**lemon slices**
1 tblsp	**chopped mixed herbs**
1 tblsp	**chopped basil**
freshly ground black pepper to taste	
1 tblsp	**flaked almonds**

Pre-heat oven to 375°F, 190°C, Gas 5

Place clean whole Strule trout on sheet of baking foil and cover well with butter, lemon juices, herbs and pepper. Place the almonds on the fish and wrap completely in the foil.

Cook in the oven for about 20 minutes or until the flesh flakes easily.

Alternatively cook in the microwave for 9-10 minutes in a covered dish (not wrapped in foil).

Transfer Strule trout to serving dish and fillet if required.

Garnish with slices of lemon.

Serve with wheaten bread and mixed green salad or boiled new potatoes and fresh green vegetables.

OMAGH GROUP, NORTHERN IRELAND REGION

Omagh Group, situated on the River Strule, was formed in 1981. The purpose-built indoor arena and clubroom were opened in 1986 and the group now have 60 riders and 28 helpers.

Cod Sauté

From Mary Peters

(Serves 4 people)

4	cod steaks
1	onion, chopped
1 clove	garlic, chopped
6oz (175g)	mushrooms, sliced
2	tomatoes, skinned & chopped
3floz (75ml)	white wine or fish stock
salt and freshly ground black pepper	
1 tblsp	toasted breadcrumbs
1 tblsp	fresh parsley, chopped

Melt the butter in the frying pan. Add the fish and fry for 10-15 minutes or until it is cooked and flakes easily. Transfer to a warmed serving dish and keep hot.

Add the onion and garlic to the pan and fry for 5 minutes. Stir in the mushrooms and tomatoes and fry for 3 minutes. Pour over the wine or stock and bring to the boil. Pour the sauce over the fish and garnish with the breadcrumbs and parsley.

MARY PETERS, CBE

Vice-President RDA. One of Northern Ireland's most successful athletes, Olympic Gold Medal winner and World record holder and triple Commonwealth Games Gold Medallist. Now very actively involved with the welfare and sports development of young people in Ulster.

Fish Mousse

(Serves 4 – 6 people)

1	tin sardines, mackerel, tuna or other fish
8oz (225g)	smooth cream cheese
1 pkt (10g)	gelatine
1	lemon, juice
2 tblsp	water
salt and freshly ground black pepper	
parsley or dill	

Process the mashed fish, cheese and only enough lemon juice to blend easily.

Soften the gelatine in the warmed water and add to the processed mixture. Mix thoroughly.

Put into ramekins or small moulds and refrigerate. Serve garnished with parsley or dill and accompanied with thin brown toast.

MRS HELEN PHILLIPS, UPTON-UPON-SEVERN GROUP, WEST MERCIA REGION

Drunken Prawns
(Prawns in whisky)

(Serves 4 people)

2oz (50g)	butter
1 medium	onion, finely chopped
8oz (225g)	peeled prawns
4	tomatoes (skinned and chopped)
4 tblsp	whisky
4 tsp	lemon juice
salt and freshly ground black pepper	
4 slices	hot toast or a little boiled rice
1 tblsp	chopped fresh parsley
4	unpeeled prawns

Melt the butter in a frying pan. Add the onion and cook very gently until soft but not coloured. Stir in the prawns and tomatoes and cook gently for 2-3 minutes. Add the whisky, lemon juice and seasoning to taste. Bring to the boil and simmer gently for 2-3 minutes.

Spoon quickly onto toast or rice. Sprinkle with parsley and garnish with unpeeled prawns.

Note – sherry or white wine may be used instead of whisky.

TISS BOMFORD, HUNTS FARM GROUP, WEST MERCIA REGION

The group was formed in 1973. They have two groups of riders, children and young adults with a variety of abilities. Some of the riders are very competitive and always make the helpers feel great, even on the most wet and miserable days!

In 1992 the group was in danger of closing due to lack of helpers, so the local TV and radio were invited to an open day and they had a wonderful response with lots of new support.

Seafood Casserole

A very appetizing and sustaining dish.

(Serves at least 8 people)

1lb (450g)	bream
1lb (450g)	haddock
1lb (450g)	monk fish
1lb (450g)	sole
1/2 bottle	white wine
1	fish stock cube
1 1/2 lb (700g)	fresh mussels
8	scallops
1medium	onion, finely chopped
3	carrots, cut in fine strips
2 sticks	celery, finely chopped
2 cloves	garlic, finely chopped (optional)
1	vegetable stock cube
14oz (400g)	tin chopped tomatoes with herbs
1/4 pt (150ml)	double cream
1 tblsp	parsley
salt and freshly ground black pepper	

Cut the fish into 2oz (50g) pieces and poach in liquid made up with half the white wine and the fish stock cube.

In a large pan place the fresh mussels with the other half of the wine. Bring to the boil and cook gently until the mussels open. Add the scallops and simmer for about 4 minutes.

Meanwhile, in a separate pan cook all the vegetables in the vegetable stock made with the cube, until they are just tender/soft.

Add the tin of chopped tomatoes to the mussels and scallops, then add the cream and seasoning. Simmer gently for about 4 minutes. Add the fish and vegetables and combine gently. Simmer for a further 2 minutes.

Serve in large soup bowls, sprinkled with chopped parsley and accompanied with chunks of French bread or wholemeal rolls.

NEW FOREST DRIVING GROUP, SOUTH REGION

Seafood Gratin

Ideal for those who are watching their weight.

(Serves 4 people)

1lb (450g)	**cod fillets (or any other fish)**
4	**spring onions**
4oz (110g)	**peeled prawns**
2	**egg yolks**
1 tsp	**cornflour**
1 tub (7oz/200g)	**low fat fromage fraiche**
1 tblsp	**parsley, chopped**
salt and freshly ground black pepper	

Cut the cod fillets into chunks. Chop the onions finely and put in a dish with the fish. Cover and microwave for 2-3 minutes on high. Add the prawns.

Beat the egg yolks with the cornflour, fromage fraiche and seasoning. Pour over the fish.

Place under a hot grill and cook until brown. Sprinkle with chopped parsley.

Serve with green vegetables.

GILL CREED, WOOKEY HOLE & WELLS GROUP, SOUTH WEST REGION

Situated in the Mendips and started in 1986 the group uses the local riding school with indoor and outdoor facilities.

They have 4 ponies of their own and hire 4 more from the school for their weekly riding sessions of three different groups aged from 8 years to middle age.

There is a hard core of capable and experienced helpers, a very cheerful and happy crowd. They are well supported by local organisations and hold an annual show in June, hard work but well worthwhile financially!

Gratin of Seafood
with Garlic Crumble

(Serves 4 – 6 people)

1 1/4 lb (550g)	haddock, skinned & filleted
4oz (110g)	peeled prawns
3/4 pt (425ml)	milk
2	bay leaves
a pinch	powdered mace
For the sauce	
1 1/2 oz (40g)	butter
1 1/2 oz (40g)	flour
1 tblsp	lemon juice
1 tblsp	oil
1 small	onion, chopped
1/2	green pepper, chopped
1 tblsp	capers (drained)
1 tblsp	parsley, chopped
salt and freshly ground black pepper	
For the topping	
4oz (110g)	breadcrumbs
2 cloves	garlic, crushed
2oz (50g)	cheese, grated
1oz (25g)	butter, cut into small dice
salt and freshly ground black pepper	

Pre-heat oven to 375°F, 190°C, Gas 5

Poach the fish in a saucepan with the milk, bay leaves, mace, salt and pepper for about 6 minutes. Remove the fish and strain the milk into a jug ready to use in the sauce.

To make the sauce – melt the butter in the same saucepan, stir in the flour. Cook. Add the reserved milk/fish liquid and lemon juice, a little at a time, stirring constantly until the sauce is smooth.

Heat the oil in a frying pan and cook the onion and green pepper until softened. Remove from the heat and set aside.

Flake the fish, mix in the prawns and place in a greased ovenproof dish, add the onion, green pepper and capers. Stir the parsley into the sauce and pour over the mixture in the casserole.

The crumble topping – mix the breadcrumbs, garlic, grated cheese and butter together. Season and then sprinkle over the top of the fish mixture. Cook in the oven for about 20 minutes or until the top is golden brown.

CHALKDOWN GROUP, SOUTH EAST REGION

Special Fish Pie

(Serves 6 – 8 people)

1lb (450g)	cod or haddock
1pkt	kipper fillets OR
6oz (175g)	smoked haddock
6oz (175g)	salmon
4oz (110g)	prawns
4oz (110g)	mussels
4	crab sticks
1 dsp	dill, finely chopped
1 dsp	parsley, finely chopped
$^1/_2$ pt (275ml)	thick white sauce (use reserved fish liquid)
1 dsp	tomato ketchup
$^1/_2$ tsp	anchovy essence
1 tsp	Worcester Sauce
1 dsp	lemon juice
salt and freshly ground black pepper	
2 dsp	creme fraiche
light and fluffy mashed potatoes, using about	
$1^1/_2$ lbs (700gms) of potatoes	

Pre-heat oven to 350°F, 180°C, Gas 4

Cook the white and smoked fish and the salmon (in the microwave). Reserving any liquid. Flake the fish (removing bones and skin) and put in a large bowl. Chop the crab sticks into chunks, and the prawns and mussels (or leave whole if you prefer). Add to the fish. Sprinkle with the dill and parsley.

Make the white sauce. Allow to cool then add the tomato ketchup, anchovy essence, Worcester Sauce and lemon juice. Season. Stir in the creme fraiche.

Fold the sauce into the fish, check and adjust seasoning if necessary.

Top with mashed potato.

To cook place in the oven for about 35 minutes. Brown the potato under the grill if necessary.

DIANA de CLERMONT, EAST LODGE FARM GROUP, NORTH MIDLANDS REGION

Tuna Tagli

An emergency meal.

(Serves 4 people)

4oz (110g)	Tagliatelle
1 10oz (295g)	can condensed cream of mushroom soup
2 tblsp	sherry medium or dry
2 tblsp	fresh parsley, chopped
1	medium onion, finely chopped
1/2 tsp	dried marjoram
6oz (185g) can	tuna
1oz (25g)	almonds, flaked
1oz (25g)	cheese, grated
salt and freshly ground black pepper	

Pre-heat oven to 350°F, 180°C, Gas 4

Cook tagliatelle as per the instructions. Drain well.

Mix all the other ingredients together (except the almonds and cheese) and then fold through the pasta.

Spoon into a greased ovenproof dish, scatter on the cheese and then the almond flakes.

Bake until golden brown, about 30 minutes.

Serve with a salad and crusty bread.

Note – diced cooked chicken can be substituted for tuna.

MRS JUNE LONG, GENNETS FARM GROUP, SOUTH EAST REGION

Tuna Fish Brunch

(Serves 6 – 8 people)

1 large	**onion, chopped**
1 tblsp	**oil**
2 tins	**baked beans**
2 tins	**tuna fish, drained**
2 tsp	**mixed herbs**
salt and freshly ground black pepper	
1 large pkt	**crisps, crushed (optional)**
6oz (175g)	**cheese, grated**

Pre-heat oven to 350°F, 180°C, Gas 4

Fry the onion in the oil until cooked but not brown.

Put the beans, tuna fish, mixed herbs and cooked onion in a greased ovenproof dish. Season if you wish. Next the crushed crisps (if you are using them) cover with grated cheese.

Put in the oven and bake until the cheese has melted and starts to turn brown.

Serve with salad and bread and butter.

MICHAEL BANBURY, a rider with CROWTHORNE GROUP, SOUTH REGION

Michael is a pupil at Ravenswood Village and Suhar David Centre for Special Education.

Quick Fish Dish

(Serves 4 people)

4 fillets	**of any white fish**
1 tin	**mushroom soup, any other soup will do, tomato is good**
salt and freshly ground black pepper	

Pre-heat oven to 375°F, 190°C, Gas 5

Take any white fish. Lay in a lightly greased ovenproof dish and season. Pour a tin of soup over.

Put in the oven until the fish is cooked.

Serve with potatoes or crusty bread to soak up the juice.

MARGARET MORGAN, BERWICKSHIRE GROUP, EDINBURGH & BORDERS REGION

Tuna and Mushroom Bake

(Serves 4 – 6 people)

1/2 lb (225g)	**frozen spinach**
1	**cauliflower (sprigged into florets)**
2 or 3	**potatoes**
1oz (25g)	**butter**
1 tblsp	**lemon juice**
6	**mushrooms**
1 large tin	**tuna**
1/2 pt (275ml)	**parsley sauce**
2oz (50g)	**breadcrumbs**
2oz (50g)	**cheddar cheese, grated**
salt and freshly ground black pepper	

Pre-heat oven to 300°F, 150°C, Gas 2

Defrost the spinach, cook the cauliflower and potatoes. Quarter the mushrooms and sauté in the butter and lemon juice.

Spread the drained spinach over the base of an ovenproof dish. Next the drained mushrooms (reserve the residue for the parsley sauce). Season lightly between layers.

Drain the tuna and spread in chunks over the mushrooms. Drain the cauliflower and add to the casserole as the next layer.

Pour the parsley sauce over. Drain the potatoes, slice them and arrange as the next layer. Finally scatter the breadcrumbs and grated cheese on top and bake for about 30 minutes.

HANFORD GROUP, SOUTH WEST REGION

Started in 1975. The weekly riding and/or stable management lessons at the indoor arena cater for 22 children of varying disabilities. The 24 helpers also run an annual gymkana. At Christmas, Father Christmas arrives on horseback but the children have to show him how to mount and ride correctly.

Yorkshire Herring Pie

(Serves 4 people)

4	**herrings**
6	**potatoes**
2	**cooking apples, peeled, chopped and dipped in mild vinegar**
	butter or bacon fat
salt and freshly ground black pepper	

Pre-heat oven to 350°F, 180°C, Gas 4

Clean the herrings and cut them into fillets. Peel the potatoes and cut them into thin slices like crisps. Arrange the potato slices round the sides and bottom of a greased ovenproof dish.

Put a layer of herring into the dish. Then a layer of apples, another layer of herrings, seasoning, and finish with potato slices as a top layer. Put a couple of knobs of butter or bacon fat on top.

Cover with greased parchment paper and a lid.

Bake for 30 minutes, remove the lid and paper and continue cooking for a further 20 minutes.

MRS MARGARET TAYLOR, WELLBURN HALL SCHOOL GROUP,
HUMBERSIDE & SOUTH YORKSHIRE REGION

Ceann Cropaig

This is a delicious stuffing for fish.

8oz (225g)	**fish liver (from cod or ling)**
8oz (225g)	**oatmeal**
2 tblsp	**flour**
salt and freshly ground black pepper	
1 medium	**onion, finely chopped, optional**

Mix the fish liver, salt and pepper until soft. Add to this the oatmeal and flour, mix until you have a stiff consistency. Add the onion if you wish it.

Stuff the head of a fish you wish to cook and boil for 40 minutes or put the mixture in a small bowl or teacup, cover and place in a large pan and boil with the fish itself.

Serve with white fish and boiled potatoes.

LEWIS AND HARRIS GROUP, GRAMPIAN AND HIGHLAND REGION

The group has been meeting once a week for the past four years. They have a break in the winter as there are no indoor or outdoor schools on the island of Lewis and the fields get too muddy. There are twelve riders and the enthusiastic helpers lend their ponies.

Soft Herring Roe Tyropitas

Serve as snacks, starters or add vegetables to make a more substantial main course.

(Serves 4 – 6 people)

8oz (225g)	**soft herring roes**
For the court bouillon	
2floz (55ml)	**white wine**
8floz (220ml)	**water**
1/2 tsp	**salt**
1 small	**onion, quartered**
1 small	**carrot, sliced**
4	**pepper corns**
	pinch thyme
	small bay leaf
1/2 pt (275ml)	**white sauce**
6	**sheets of filo pastry**
2oz (50g)	**butter, melted**

Pre-heat oven to 375°F, 190°C, Gas 5.

Put all the ingredients for the court bouillon into a pan, bring to the boil and simmer gently for 15 minutes. Leave to cool. Strain the cool court bouillon over the herring roes and bring to the boil. Simmer very gently for 10 minutes and leave to cool. Remove roes from the liquid and pat dry.

Meanwhile make the white sauce. Remove any dark membranes from the roes. Chop up and mix with the white sauce. Adjust the seasoning.

Cut each sheet of pastry into two and keep it moist under a damp cloth.

Divide herring roe mixture into twelve portions. Paint half the sheet of pastry with melted butter and fold into three lengthwise. Then place one portion of filling on one end/corner of the pastry, spreading it to make a triangle.

Then fold the triangle over several times (about 6 – 8) triangularly until you reach the end. Seal the edges. Repeat with the other portion.

Place all 12 triangles on a buttered baking tray. Brush with butter and cook for about 30 minutes or until golden brown.

MRS S A DERBYSHIRE, BARNSTAPLE AND DISTRICT GROUP, SOUTH WEST REGION

meat – poultry – game

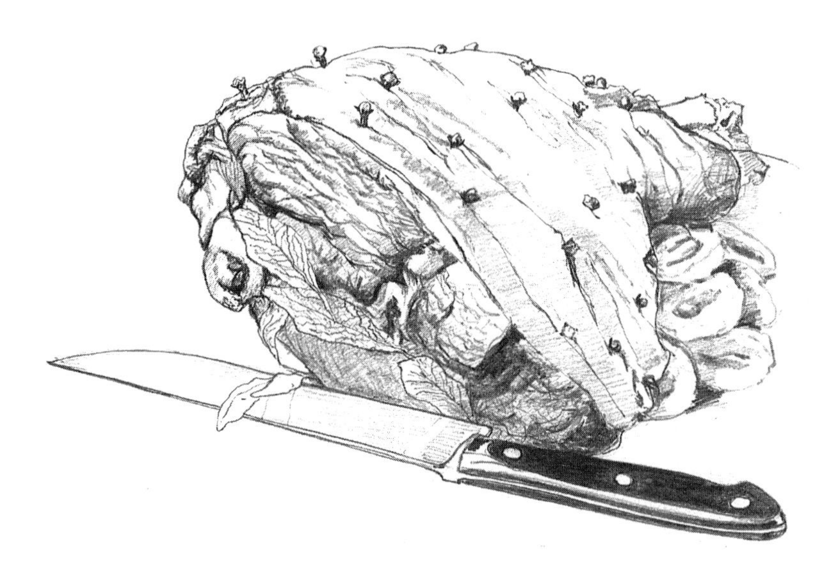

Hunters Schnitzel

(Serves 6 – 8 people)

3lbs ($1^1/_2$ kg)	**fillet beef (or veal)**
4oz (110g)	**butter**
8oz (225g)	**small capped mushrooms**
2 tblsp	**whisky**
$^1/_2$ pt (275ml)	**beef stock**
$^1/_2$ pt (275ml)	**double cream (optional)**
salt and freshly ground black pepper	

Cut the meat into individual steaks. Season. Melt the butter in a fireproof casserole until hot and seal the steaks very quickly. Remove from the pan and keep hot.

Trim 6 or 8 mushroom caps and keep whole. Cook lightly in pan, then remove and reserve. Roughly chop the remainder and sauté in the butter. Then add the whisky and stock, return the meat to the mixture, add the cream and simmer until the meat is tender.

Place steaks on hot plates, arrange mushroom caps on top, and pour the pan juices over. Serve with chopped mushrooms and potatoes and green vegetables.

HUMBERSIDE AND SOUTH YORKSHIRE REGION

Cantonese Steak

Recipe for a delicious stew. Excellent after a long day's driving as it can be left in a very low oven all day.

(Serves 6 – 8 people)

3lbs ($1^1/2$ kg)	**shin of beef, cubed OR chuck steak (a more expensive version!)**
1 pt (570ml)	**water**
For the marinade	
2floz (55ml)	**soy sauce**
2floz (55ml)	**sherry (or rice wine)**
2 tblsp	**soft brown sugar**
$^1/_2$ tsp	**cinnamon**
$^1/_2$ bottle	**red wine (optional, for the more expensive version!)**
2 tblsp	**cornflour**
salt and freshly ground black pepper	

Mix all the above ingredients (except the cornflour) and marinate the meat for 4-12 hours.

Pre-heat oven to 275°F, 140°C, Gas 1 or less.

Then place meat, marinade and water in an ovenproof casserole and cook slowly for $2^1/_2$-3 hours.

Next mix the cornflour with a little cold water and stir into the stew, to thicken it. Re-heat, adjust seasoning and serve with plain boiled rice or **ginger rice.**

Ginger rice

Sauté chopped onion, chives and chopped preserved ginger, add to the cooked rice to taste.

EAST REGION DRIVING

Pepper Beef Casserole

(Serves 4 – 6 people)

1oz (25g)	flour
salt and freshly ground black pepper	
$^1/_2$ tsp	ground ginger
2lbs (900g)	braising steak, cubed
2oz (50g)	dripping (or oil and butter)
1	red pepper, de-seed and sliced
For the sauce	
1tsp	hot chilli sauce
14oz (400g)	can tomatoes
4oz (110g)	mushrooms, sliced
1 tblsp	Worcester Sauce
2 tblsp	wine vinegar
2 cloves	garlic, crushed
1	bay leaf

Pre-heat oven to 325°F, 170°C, Gas 3

Mix together the flour, seasoning and ginger and coat the beef by tossing in the flour.

Heat the dripping (oil) in a large heavy bottomed pan. Add the beef and brown quickly. Drain and transfer to an ovenproof casserole.

For the sauce combine all the ingredients and pour over the meat. Cover and cook for about 2 hours or until meat is tender.

WARMINSTER GROUP, MID-WEST REGION

From David Broome, OBE

Yorkshire Pudding

to accompany his favourite menu

Roast Sirloin of Beef
(medium rare)
with Yorkshire Pudding
Green Vegetables
Roast Potatoes
Gravy
Horseradish Sauce
Creme Brûlée

A very traditional British meal from a very traditional Yorkshire man!

Wine Recommendation

Nothing can beat the classic combination of claret with roast beef. Michel Lynch Bordeaux Rouge 89/90 is excellent value.

To make the Yorkshire Pudding

4oz (110g)	plain flour
1/4 tsp	salt
1	egg
1/2 pt (275ml)	milk
2 tblsp	hot dripping from the roast of meat

Sieve the flour and salt into a bowl. Make a well in the centre. Drop in the egg and stir in half the milk.

Stir until smooth, then beat the batter well until air bubbles rise. Stir in the rest of the milk, cover the batter, and let it stand for an hour.

Next put about 2 tablespoons of hot dripping from the roast of meat into a Yorkshire tin (or individual "bun" tins). Pour in the batter and bake in a hot oven, (400°F, 200°C, Gas 6), with the roast for about 20 minutes.

When brown, well risen and sufficiently cooked, cut the pudding into about 8 pieces and serve on a hot dish.

DAVID BROOME OBE

Vice-President of RDA. One of Britain's most consistently successful show jumpers. His exceptional career includes winning the European Show Jumping Championship 3 times as well as the World Show Jumping Championship in 1970.

Home Spiced Beef

This is a particularly good dish over the Christmas season, as a change from the Turkey. But don't forget you need to start 11 days in advance!

5lb (2 1/2 kg)	piece of silverside
3oz (75g)	soft dark brown sugar
4oz (100g)	rock or sea salt
1oz (25g)	allspice powder
10 whole cloves garlic – roughly crushed	
3	bay leaves
a good grating of nutmeg	
10oz (25g)	black peppercorns

Place beef in a deep non-metallic dish. Rub all over with the sugar, cover with greaseproof paper and then a sheet of foil. Leave in a cool place for 2 days, re-rubbing after 24 hours.

Then mix salt, spices, nutmeg and garlic together, rub into the beef all over, add bay leaves on top and cover as before.

Repeat rubbing process daily for nine days. The smell is wonderful!

Then remove beef from its liquid and wipe off adhering spices with damp kitchen paper.

To cook – Pre-heat oven to 275°F, 140°C, Gas 1

Place meat in a snugly fitting casserole, add 1/2 pt (275ml) of water only. Cover with 3 layers of foil and the lid. Cook for 4 1/2 hours.

To serve slice thinly. Absolutely delicious hot with dumplings, carrots, etc. and equally good (allow the beef to cool in its own cooking liquid) used cold with pickles and crusty bread or in sandwiches.

PAT AUSTIN STONE, THE JILLIAN RAYMOND GROUP, (FORMERLY GREEN HEDGES GROUP), EAST REGION

The Jillian Raymond Group is named in memory of their late Chairman. They have 20 children and 10 adult riders all mentally handicapped who ride in the indoor arena and also on the paths and fields. They have an annual holiday on the Norfolk coast, taking eight children, five ponies, a trap and helpers, all enjoy riding on the beach.

Lamb with Rosemary
Casserole

(Serves 4 people)

4	lamb chops
2 medium	onions
2	carrots
2 tsp	rosemary, dried or fresh
1/4 pt (150ml)	tomato juice
1/2 tblsp	tomato puree
3/4 pt (425ml)	water
dash	Worcester Sauce
salt and freshly ground black pepper	
1 dsp	cornflour

Pre-heat oven to 300°F, 150°C, Gas 2

Peel and chop the onions and carrots and place in the casserole. Lay the chops on top of the vegetables.

Mix together the tomato juice, puree, water, Worcester Sauce and seasoning. Pour over the meat and vegetables and cook for 1 3/4 hours.

Mix the cornflour with a little water and add to the casserole to thicken. Cook for a further 15 minutes.

Serve with baked potatoes and green vegetables.

CHRISTINE JONES, HEREFORD GROUP, WEST MERCIA REGION

Baked Lamb
with Pears

(Serves 4 – 8 people)

8	lamb chops
1 tblsp	oil
2	pears, just ripe
1/2 pt (275ml)	apple juice
1 tblsp	fresh marjoram, finely chopped OR
1 tsp	dried marjoram
2 tblsp	lemon juice
salt and freshly ground black pepper	

Pre-heat oven to 375°F, 190°C, Gas 5

Season the lamb and in a frying pan brown the chops in hot oil on both sides. Remove and place in an ovenproof casserole. Peel core and thickly slice the pears, fry for 1 minute, then drain on kitchen paper, and add to the chops.

Add the apple juice to the pan, together with the marjoram (reserve a little for garnish) and lemon juice. Boil rapidly for 2-3 minutes to reduce. Pour the sauce over the lamb and pears. Cover and cook for 20-30 minutes. Garnish with marjoram sprinkled over.

ALICE SUMMERHAYS, ISLE OF WIGHT GROUP, SOUTH REGION

The island group was started 21 years ago with the Driving Group formed in 1981. The two groups function separately but keep in close contact.

Lamb Chops
with Barbecue Sauce

(Serves 4 people)

4	**Lamb chops, loin or chump**
salt and freshly ground black pepper	
1oz (25g)	**butter**
1 small	**onion, chopped**
4 tblsp	**tomato ketchup**
2 tblsp	**vinegar**
2 tblsp	**soft brown sugar**
1 tsp	**made mustard**
1 tblsp	**Worcester Sauce**

Pre-heat oven to 400°F, 200°C, Gas 6

Season the chops and arrange in a shallow roasting tin. Roast for 10 minutes in the centre of oven.

Meanwhile prepare the sauce. In a saucepan melt the butter, add the onion and sauté till tender, about 5 minutes. Add the remaining ingredients to the pan, mix well. Gradually bring to the boil, stirring all the while. Remove from the heat.

Remove the chops from the oven and reduce the temperature to 375°F, 190°C, Gas 5.

Drain off any fat from the chops, pour the barbecue sauce over the chops, return to the oven and continue to cook for a further 20-30 minutes, basting frequently.

SHEELAGH BENHAM, LISBURN GROUP, NORTHERN IRELAND REGION

Honey and Orange Glazed Lamb Chops

Serves 4 people)

4	lamb chops
2 tblsp	seasoned flour
1oz (10g)	butter
1 tblsp	cooking oil
3	oranges
1 tblsp	honey
1 tblsp	fresh mint, finely chopped OR
1 tsp	dried mint
salt and freshly ground black pepper	

Trim any excess fat from the chops and coat with the seasoned flour. Melt the butter with the oil in the frying pan and on a moderate heat brown the chops on both sides. Meanwhile finely pare the rind of one orange and cut into fine julienne strips. Reserve $^1/_2$ for garnish. Juice the two oranges and add enough water to make $^1/_2$ pint (275ml).

To the pan add the juice, half the julienne strips, the honey and the mint. Blend well. Reduce the heat, cover and simmer gently for 20-30 minutes (depending on how you like your lamb cooked).

Remove the chops and keep warm in a serving dish. Skim off any fat from the sauce and then reduce the sauce until it is thick and syrupy. Adjust the seasoning. Pour the sauce over the chops and garnish with the reserved julienne of orange, orange cartwheels (if you wish) and (cut from the third orange) slices. Serve with sprigs of fresh mint.

JENNIFER FORREST, DUNS GROUP, EDINBURGH & BORDERS REGION

Pork Tenderloin

with Cheese & Tomato

A wonderful colour scheme.

(Serves 6 – 8 people)

2	pork tenderloins (left whole)
3/4 pt (425ml)	stock with a dash of wine or orange juice
a piece of	celery, carrot and onion
2	slices bacon
8oz (225g)	Edam or Gruyere cheese, sliced
12	small shallots (skinned but whole)
14oz (400g)	can chopped tomatoes
2 tblsp	olive oil
1/2 oz (10g)	butter
pinch	sugar
salt and freshly ground black pepper	
1 dsp	mixed herbs
salt and freshly ground black pepper	

Pre-heat oven to 375°F, 190°C, Gas 5

Place the pork tenderloins in a roasting pan, add the stock. Coarsely chop the celery, carrot and onion and place around the meat. Put a slice of bacon on each tenderloin.

Cook uncovered for first 10 minutes then cover and cook for a further 20-30 minutes (depending on the size and weight of the tenderloin).

When cooked take out and cut into slices about 1/4 inch (1/2 cm) thick. Cook the shallots in the olive oil, butter and sugar. Place in a shallow fireproof dish together with the can of chopped tomatoes. Assemble the tenderloin into its original shape with a slice of cheese between each slice. Spoon some of the tomato sauce over it. Season and sprinkle with herbs.

Return to the oven and re-heat.

Serve with mashed potato and a green salad or green cooked vegetables.

JOSEPHINE GARDNER, WELLINGTON GROUP, SOUTH REGION

Pork Basil Brush

(Serves 4 – 6 people)

$1^1/_4$ lbs (560g)	pork fillet
1	small onion, chopped
4 tblsp	olive oil
$^1/_4$ tsp	basil, dried
$^1/_4$ tsp	sage, dried
$^1/_8$ tsp	dill, dried
6 tblsp	port
3 tblsp	flour
1pt (570ml)	meat stock
salt and freshly ground black pepper	

Pre-heat oven to 275°F, 140°C, Gas 1

Trim the meat and cut into $^1/_2$" (1 cm) slices. Cook the onion in a heavy bottomed frying pan with 2 tablespoons of olive oil until transparent. Add the herbs and 2 tablespoons of the port, cook for a further 2 minutes. Put into an ovenproof casserole.

Coat the pork slices in seasoned flour, and brown in the remaining olive oil. Place the meat in the casserole, add the stock and 2 more tablespoons of port. Cover.

Cook for about $1^1/_2$ hours. 5 minutes before serving add the final 2 tablespoons port.

NICKY FORBES, ABERDEEN GROUP, HIGHLAND & GRAMPIAN REGION

Squab Pie

A good way of using left over roast lamb.
Bramley apples give best results.

	Sliced, cold cooked lamb
1 medium	onion per person
2 medium	cooking apples per person
2 tblsp	brown sugar per person
	salt and freshly ground black pepper
	stock

Pre-heat oven to 350°F, 180°C, Gas 4

Peel and slice the apples and onions and arrange in layers in a casserole dish, cover with brown sugar, then add a layer of sliced lamb, then onion, etc. Continue up the pot finishing with the apple at the top. Season. Add stock – enough to almost cover the top. Cover casserole with a well fitting lid and cook for about $1^1/_2$ hours.

HOLTWOOD GROUP, SOUTH WEST REGION

Apple & Prune Stuffing
with Pork

(Serves 4 – 6 people)

4 - 6 chops or 3lb (approx 1½ kg) boned, rolled joint

For the stuffing

1lb (450g)	apples, peeled, cored and chopped,
4oz (110g)	prunes, cooked, stoned and chopped
6oz (175g)	fresh white breadcrumbs
1oz (25g)	flaked almonds, toasted
1 tblsp	onion, grated
1 tblsp	fresh thyme OR
1 tsp	dried thyme
2oz (50g)	butter
a little milk	
Salt and freshly ground black pepper	

Pre-heat oven to 400°F, 200°C, Gas 6

To make the stuffing

Melt the butter, place all the other ingredients except the milk in a bowl. Pour the melted butter into the mixture and stir. Add just enough milk to bind. Bake separately in an ovenproof dish for 20-30 minutes and serve with the pork, or use to stuff a rolled joint.

CHALKDOWN GROUP, SOUTH EAST REGION

Raisin Sauce

To serve with baked ham.

½ pt (275ml)	water
8oz (225g)	sugar
8oz (225g)	raisins
2 tblsp	butter
2 tblsp	vinegar
½ tsp	salt
8oz (225g)	grape or redcurrant jelly
4	cloves
½ tsp	cinnamon
2 tsp	cornflour

In a heavy bottomed saucepan mix the sugar and water and bring to the boil. Add the raisins, butter, vinegar, salt, jelly, cloves and cinnamon. Stir well and return to the boil.

Mix the cornflour with a little cold water. Add to the sauce stirring continuously until the mixture thickens, but don't make it too stiff.

Delicious served with boiled or baked ham.

FRANCES JOHNSTON, ENNISKILLEN GROUP, NORTHERN IRELAND REGION

From Peter Scudamore

Duck Roast in Orange Sauce

As served in the Black Horse Inn, Naunton, nr Cheltenham, Glos., by Jenny Bowen-Jones.

(Serves 4 people)

4	large Duck Breasts, skinned
$1^1/_2$ oz (40g)	unsalted butter
2 tblsp	orange marmalade
1 tblsp	lemon juice, freshly squeezed
2 tblsp	mandarin liqueur
1	orange, the zest
	parsley, chopped

Melt the butter in a frying pan. When it stops foaming add the duck breasts and brown well each side.

Put the duck breasts under the grill until cooked through.

For the sauce, mix the marmalade, lemon juice and liqueur in a saucepan. Add the zest of orange at the end when it is runny.

Pour the hot sauce over the duck, making sure the zest lies on top of the breasts.

Garnish with chopped parsley.

PETER SCUDAMORE MBE

Vice-President, RDA. In an outstanding career as one of Britains's leading National Hunt jockeys, he set a new record for the number of winners ridden in a career, and together with trainer Martin Pipe formed one of the most brilliant partnerships in National Hunt racing.

From Henry Cecil

Crispy Roast Duck
with sliced Avocado Salad

"A couple of very quick recipes which I particularly enjoy."

1	duck
1 tblsp	salt
1	avocado
1	crispy lettuce (Iceberg)
1	sweet grapefruit
Good French or Italian dressing	

Pre-heat oven to 400°F, 200°C, Gas 6

Wash and clean out the duck. Dry thoroughly. Make several cuts into the surface of the upper skin of the duck.

Place in a roasting dish. Rub with salt. Cover with foil and cook for 30 minutes to the 1lb. 25 minutes before the cooking time ends, uncover the duck and return to the oven to crisp.

To make the sliced avocado salad, peel the avocado, halve and take the stone out. Lay each half hole side down on a bed of shredded lettuce. Partially slice through the top of the pear without dividing it. Halve a sweet grapefruit and extract segments without pith or stones, place over and around the avocado and serve with a good French or Italian dressing.

HENRY CECIL

One of the outstanding trainers in the history of the flat. Ten times champion trainer, his record includes 3 Derby winners and 3 Oaks winners.

Among the great horses trained at Warren Place have been St Paddy, Reference Point, Slip Anchor, Crepolla, Petit Etoile and many more.

Susse Spatchcocks

Spatchcock is a term applied to small birds split down the back and flattened. Eels may be treated in the same way. They are called Spitchcocks.

(Serves 4 people)

2 spatchcocks OR	
4 chicken pieces	
2 tblsp	**oil**
1/2 bottle	**white wine**
6oz (175g)	**Gruyere cheese, grated**
1/2 pt (275ml)	**sour cream**
1 dsp	**Dijon mustard**
salt and freshly ground black pepper	
watercress to garnish	

Pre-heat oven to 375°F, 190°F, 5 Gas

Brush the spatchcocks/chicken pieces with oil and place in a casserole and roast for 20-30 minutes, or until cooked. Remove the spatchcock/chicken pieces.

Then put the fireproof casserole on top of the hob, add the wine and half the grated cheese, gradually bring to the boil, stirring well and continually scraping the sides. Add the sour cream and Dijon mustard. Adjust seasoning.

Return spatchcock/chicken pieces to the sauce, sprinkle with the remainder of the cheese and brown under the grill.

Serve traditionally garnished with watercress.

MID-SUSSEX GROUP, SOUTH EAST REGION

Chicken and Mushroom Parcels

(Serves 4 people)

4 tblsp	**tomato puree**
2 tblsp	**white wine**
2 tsp	**garlic puree or granules**
4 tsp	**hot paprika**
salt and freshly ground black pepper	
4	**chicken joints, skinned**
4	**potatoes, pan-boiled and sliced**
8oz (225g)	**onion, sliced**
4oz (110g)	**mushrooms, sliced**
2oz (50g)	**butter**

Pre-heat oven to 350°F, 180°C, Gas 4

Cut 4 large, double thickness squares of baking foil, enough to make a roomy parcel for each joint. Also a piece of parchment paper to line the foil.

In a bowl make a soft paste/thick sauce by mixing the tomato puree, wine, garlic and paprika together.

Season each joint. Place potato and onion slices in the centre of a square of foil or parchment. Coat each chicken joint in the tomato paste mixture, and place on top of the potato and onion. Cover with slices of mushroom. Place a knob of butter on top of each joint.

Seal the foil parcels. Place on a baking sheet and cook in the oven for about 1 hour.

Serve with salad or vegetables.

LANJETH GROUP, SOUTH WEST REGION

The group started in 1975. They ride 1-2 hours, 4 days a week, 40 weeks of the year with 65 riders and 25 helpers. They use excellent indoor and outdoor facilities of the Lanjeth Riding School which offers a full range of instruction. When funds permit they are planning to add driving.

Swedish Chicken Salad

(Serves 6 – 8 people)

$3^1/_2$ lb ($1^1/_2$ kg) roast chicken	
6oz (175g)	**white/brown rice**
1	**green eating apple**
2	**bananas**
1 tblsp	**lemon juice**
$^1/_4$ pt (150ml)	**double cream**
3floz (75ml)	**mayonnaise**
1 tsp	**curry powder**
salt and freshly ground black pepper	
watercress to garnish	

Carve the chicken and cut into 1" ($2^1/_2$ cm) strips. Cook the rice and cool.

Core and thinly slice the apples and the bananas. Toss the fruit in the lemon juice.

Whip the cream until it is the consistency of mayonnaise and combine it with the mayonnaise, add the curry powder.

Fold in the chicken, apple, bananas, add more lemon juice and adjust seasoning if desired.

Serve right away on a bed of rice, garnished with watercress. Serve with a salad.

RHINS OF GALLOWAY GROUP, EDINBURGH AND BORDERS REGION

Started in 1982 this group now has 18 riders and a waiting list. They only ride outside from April to September and the money received from the BBC's Children in Need appeal in 1991 has enabled them to have an all weather surface, lovely under the feet in the wet weather!

Supreme of Chicken Glendun

Taken step by step this is very attractive and effective.

(Serves 2 people)

2 x 3-4oz (75-110g)	**chicken breasts**
1oz (25g)	**smoked salmon (2 slices)**
1oz (25g)	**prawns**
$^{1}/_{2}$ oz (10g)	**butter (softened)**
2	**spinach leaves**
salt and freshly ground black pepper	
$^{1}/_{2}$ pt (275ml)	**chicken stock**
For the sauce	
$^{1}/_{2}$ oz (10g)	**butter**
2oz (50g)	**mushrooms, thinly sliced**
1 glass	**white wine**
1 tblsp	**cream**
1 tblsp	**yoghurt**

Pre-heat oven to 400°F, 200°C, Gas 6

Remove the skin from the chicken breasts. Separate the fillets, and beat out both breasts and fillets. Blanche the spinach leaves in a little boiling water and refresh in cold water.

Chop the prawns, mix with the butter and place onto the two slices of smoked salmon.

Place the two chicken breasts flat on the table, presentation side down. Place the spinach leaves on top and on top of that the smoked salmon, spread with prawns. Next the chicken fillets. Season if you wish. Roll up to make a sort of cone, i.e. one end is smaller than the other.

Butter 2 pieces of tin foil and wrap these around the cones, quite tightly. The chicken is now ready for cooking. To cook place in an earthenware dish, add the chicken stock, place in the oven, cook for 15 minutes, remove from the oven. Open the foil and check the chicken is cooked – add the juices to the stock, keep the chicken hot.

Meanwhile make the sauce – melt the butter in a saucepan, add the sliced mushrooms, cook gently. Add the wine, the cream, the chicken stock, adjust the seasoning and when ready to serve add the yoghurt. Do not boil.

To serve – slice each chicken cone and arrange on the plate, serve the sauce separately. The suggested vegetables are Parisienne potatoes and carrot bundles (matchsticks of carrots tied with a strip of leek and lightly cooked).

This recipe was created by DAVID SANDS JNR. (aged 10),
FORT GROUP, NORTHERN IRELAND REGION

From Mrs Sheila M Shaw

Chicken with Artichoke Hearts

"Easy and everyone seems to like it, but doesn't know what's in it!"

(Serves 6 – 8 people)

For the base

2 x 15g (400g)	tin artichoke hearts (or broccoli)
1 1/2 lbs (700g)	cooked chicken (cut up roughly)
2 x 10oz (275g)	tin chicken soup, condensed
6oz (175g)	mayonnaise
1 tsp	curry powder
2 tsp	lemon juice
freshly ground black pepper	
4oz (110g)	cheddar cheese, grated
6 slices	thick white bread, cubed
2oz (50g)	butter, melted

Pre-heat oven to 375°F, 190°C, Gas 5

Drain and quarter the artichoke hearts and together with the chopped cooked chicken place in the bottom of a casserole.

Mix together the condensed chicken soup, mayonnaise, curry powder, lemon juice and black pepper and spoon over the chicken mixture.

Top this with the grated cheese.

Next toss the croutons in the melted butter until it is all absorbed and arrange, uncooked, over the cheese.

Cook for 45-50 minutes until thoroughly heated through and crisp on top.

MRS SHEILA SHAW

Honorary Life Vice-President RDA. Founded a number of the original RDA groups and helped to set up many others. With the late Kay Moseley produced the first film, *Riding for the Disabled*. Served on the Council 1969-84. Has also been a fundraiser, an instructor and dressage judge.

Chicken with Cheshire Cheese & Lemon Sauce

(Serves 4 people)

4	chicken breasts
1 tblsp	sherry
1 tblsp	lemon juice
1 tsp	grated lemon rind
1/4 pt (150ml)	single cream
3oz (75g)	white Cheshire cheese

Pre-heat oven to 350°F, 180°C, Gas 4

Cook the chicken pieces until tender. (Grill or bake for 20-30 minutes). Keep the pieces warm.

Heat the sherry, juice and rind in a pan, and slowly add the cream. Do not allow to boil.

Place the chicken breasts in a fireproof dish. Pour the sauce over them, then cover with crumbled cheese and grill until brown and bubbly.

MRS G MANNIA, MID CHESHIRE GROUP, NORTH WEST REGION

Chicken with Coriander & Kumquats

(Serves 4 – 6 people)

2 tblsp	oil
8	chicken thighs
1 large	clove garlic
1	orange, zest and juice
1/4 pt (150ml)	chicken stock
2floz (55ml)	dry white wine
4oz (110g)	kumquats, halved
3 tblsp	fresh coriander, chopped
salt and freshly ground black pepper	

Heat the oil in a large fireproof casserole. Brown the chicken thighs on all sides. Add the garlic clove, grated zest of orange, orange juice, the stock and wine. Mix well. Bring to the boil. Cover and simmer for 15 minutes.

Add the kumquats and coriander, stir. Continue simmering uncovered, for a further 20 minutes.

Adjust the seasoning, remove the garlic clove and serve.

TWINSTEAD GROUP, EAST REGION

Chicken in Cider

(Serves 4 – 6 people)

1 tblsp	oil
4oz (110g)	butter
3lb (1 1/2 kg)	chicken, portioned
1 medium	onion, peeled and sliced
1oz (25g)	flour
3/4 pt (425ml)	cider
3/4 pt (425ml)	stock
1 tsp	dried mixed herbs
salt and freshly ground black pepper	
2lbs (900g)	bramleys, peeled, cored and sliced

Pre-heat oven to 350°F, 180°C, Gas 4

Heat the oil and half the butter in a frying pan and brown the chicken portions. Remove and put into a casserole. Add the onions to the fat and cook until soft, add the flour, and allow to go a golden brown. Gradually add the cider, stock and herbs, bring to the boil. Season the sauce and pour over the chicken. Cover and cook in the oven for 1 hour.

Cook the apple rings in the remaining butter for approximately 1 minute per side until pale gold. Place on top of the chicken to serve. Will freeze.

CHALKDOWN GROUP, SOUTH EAST REGION

Cream Curried Chicken Breasts

(Serves 4 – 6 people)

6 fillets	chicken breasts
2oz (50g)	butter
2 tsp	curry powder
2floz (55ml)	whisky
1 clove	garlic, crushed
salt and freshly ground black pepper	
1	orange, zest of
1/4 pt (150ml)	cream

Cut the chicken into strips. Melt the butter and fry the chicken strips gently until cooked. Remove and keep warm.

Sprinkle in the curry powder (to taste) and blend in well. Then add the garlic salt and pepper and the zest of orange. Pour the whisky over and ignite. Next stir in the cream and allow the sauce to simmer for 5 minutes. Pour the sauce over the chicken.

ANNE REID, MARKINGTON GROUP, YORKSHIRE & CLEVELAND REGION

The group has recently celebrated its 21st birthday. The riders, physically and mentally handicapped come from two local Barnado's schools and four adults also join in the term time rides. They also have use of an indoor arena provided weekly by a local family.

Chicken Pie

(Serves 4 – 6 people)

12oz (350g)	**short crust pastry**
8oz (225g)	**cooked chicken**
1 small	**onion, finely chopped**
1oz (25g)	**butter**
2	**eggs**
4floz (110ml)	**milk**
salt and freshly ground black pepper	

Pre-heat oven to 375°F, 190°C, Gas 5

Melt the butter and gently cook the onion until transparent, allow to cool.

Line a greased 8" (20cm) pie plate/dish with the short crust pastry. Roll out enough for the lid, reserve. Whisk the eggs and milk, add the seasoning, and then add the chicken and onion and fill the pastry case, reserving a little of the liquid to brush the pastry top.

Place the lid on the pie, sealing the edges carefully, brush the top and cut a small cross as an air hole. Bake for about 45 minutes. Serve hot or cold.

MRS M A YATES, THE MACHARS GROUP, EDINBURGH AND BORDERS REGION

Chicken Stuffing

(Enough to stuff one chicken)

1 small	**leek, thinly sliced**
2 sticks	**celery, thinly sliced**
1/2 oz (10g)	**butter**
1	**lemon zest and juice**
1 thick slice	**brown bread, crumbed**
1oz (25g)	**walnuts, chopped**
1oz (25g)	**raisins**
salt and freshly ground black pepper	
Parsley and chives, fresh if possible	

Add 2 tablespoons of water and the butter to the leeks and celery. Microwave on high for 2-3 minutes. Do not drain. Add lemon rind, juice, breadcrumbs, walnuts and raisins. Mix well. Season to taste and add herbs as required.

HANFORD GROUP, SOUTH WEST REGION

From Robert Smith

Chicken Curry

1 large	onion, chopped
1 large	cooking apple, chopped
1oz (25g)	butter
1 tblsp	flour
$1^1/_2$ tblsp	mild curry powder
1 pt (570ml)	chicken stock
1	lemon, the juice
2 tblsp	mango chutney
1 tblsp	brown sauce
large handful	sultanas
large handful	desiccated coconut
1	roast chicken, off the bone and shredded
1	banana
2-3 tblsp	double cream
salt and freshly ground black pepper	

Fry the onion and apple in butter and add the flour and the curry powder, continue cooking for about 1 minute.

Gradually stir in the stock and bring to the boil. Add the lemon juice, chutney, brown sauce, sultanas and coconut, blend well and continue to simmer. Stir in the shredded cooked chicken and simmer gently for about 1 hour.

Just before serving add the cream and sliced banana, taste and adjust seasoning.

Serve with rice.

ROBERT SMITH

One of the UK's leading show jumpers. As son of Harvey Smith a worthy successor in a family tradition of equestrian excellence.

Turkey with Mango

(Serves 4 people)

1oz (10g)	butter
1lb (450g)	turkey breasts, sliced
1	fresh mango OR
14oz (440g)	tin mango
1/2 pt (275ml)	double cream
1 tblsp	parsley, chopped or sprigged for garnish

Pre-heat oven to 375°F, 190°C, Gas 5

Beat the turkey breasts to tenderize if necessary. Melt butter and brown the turkey slices on both sides. Place in an ovenproof casserole. Slice the mango and with all the juice (even if you are using tinned mango) add to the turkey slices. Cover and bake for about 30 minutes until the turkey is cooked. Remove the mango pieces and juice. Keep the turkey warm.

Reserve 1 piece of mango per portion and keep warm. Put the remaining mango and juice in the processor and whizz until smooth. Reheat in a pan, add the cream, adjust the seasoning.

Serve the turkey covered in the creamy mango sauce, top with a slice of mango and garnish with the parsley.

FEN END GROUP, WEST MERCIA REGION

Turkey/ Chicken Bake

Unanimously requested and enjoyed at the Saxon groups social gatherings.

(Serves 6 – 8 people)

2 1/2 lb (1 1/4 kg)	turkey or chicken, boned & skinless
1 medium	onion, finely chopped
1	green pepper, diced
1 tin 10oz (225g)	condensed chicken soup
1/4 pt (150ml)	mayonnaise
salt and freshly ground black pepper	
For the topping	
4oz (110g)	grated cheese
4oz (110g)	crushed cornflakes

Pre-heat oven to 375°F, 190°C, Gas 5

Fry the onions, add the turkey and cook. When cool enough chop the turkey. Mix together with the mayonnaise and condensed soup. Season and put in an ovenproof dish.

Mix the cheese and cornflakes and spread on top of the turkey mixture.

Bake for 40 minutes.

SAXON GROUP, MID-WEST REGION

Started 13 years ago the group now has 25 adult riders and 24 helpers. They are fortunate to have the use of an indoor school and 5 ponies for their weekly sessions.

From The Countess of Swinton

Casserole of Pheasant
with Chestnuts

(Serves 2 – 4 people)

1	pheasant
1oz (25g)	butter
1 tblsp	olive oil
1/2 lb (225g)	chestnuts (weighed when peeled & skinned)
1/2 lb (225g)	button onions
1 tblsp	flour
1pt (570ml)	good stock
1/2	orange, grated rind & juice
1 dsp	redcurrant jelly
1 tsp	red wine vinegar OR
1 glass	burgundy
a bouquet garni	
salt and freshly ground black pepper	
1 tblsp	parsley, chopped

Pre-heat oven to 325°F, 170°C, Gas 3

Brown the pheasant slowly all over in the hot butter or oil. Remove from the pan. Sauté the chestnuts and onions briskly until they begin to change colour, shaking the pan frequently. Remove from the pan and add enough flour to take up the remaining fat. Mix well.

Add the rest of the ingredients (except the parsley) and bring to the boil. Return the pheasant to the casserole, surround with the chestnuts and onions and cover tightly.

Cook in the oven for 1 1/2 – 2 hours.

Remove the bird and joint it. Place in a deep serving dish with the chestnuts and onions. Remove the bouquet garni, skim the liquor and reduce if necessary. Adjust the seasoning.

Pour the sauce over the pheasant, dust with chopped parsley and serve.

SUSAN SWINTON, COUNTESS OF SWINTON

Honorary Life Vice-President RDA. Paralysed by a riding accident, she took her seat in the House of Lords and has championed many activities for the disabled including riding. She also breeds Highland Ponies.

From Lt Col Sir John Miller, GCVO, DSO, MC

A Winter Menu

When the days begin to shorten and the nights are drawing in, the best evenings are spent in the comfort of one's own home.

There are few things to compare with indulging in a good meal with a group of friends and a bottle of fine port.
At Shotover Park, the beautiful Oxfordshire home of Sir John Miller, Vice President of the RDA and retired Crown Equerry, pheasants are a favourite item on the menu. Shot on the estate, the birds are traditionally hung in the old game larder until reaching their prime whereupon they are taken and prepared for the table. Sir John Miller has kindly provided the following Winter Menu courtesy of his Housekeeper, Mrs Jennifer Meier.

MENU

Eggs Connaught
Shotover Pheasant with Grapes
Broccoli
Wild Rice
Chocolate Mousse with Raspberries
Viennese Biscuits

Shotover Pheasant with Black Grapes

2	pheasants (plucked and drawn)
2oz (50g)	butter
3 tblsp	brandy
12oz (350g)	black grapes
8floz (250ml)	red wine
4floz (120ml)	stock (tinned consomme can also be used)

Preheat the oven to 350°F, 180°C, Gas 4

Using a flame proof casserole dish, brown the pheasants slowly on all sides in the butter.

Flame with the brandy then take out the pheasants. Add the grapes, saving a handful for decoration at the end. Cook the grapes over a gentle heat, turning and crushing them well.

Add the wine and stock and mix in. Add the pheasants. Cover and cook in oven for 35-45 minutes.

Joint the pheasants into portions and garnish with the remaining grapes. Serve with wild rice, flaked almonds and celery plus steamed broccoli.

Eat and enjoy!

LT COL SIR JOHN MILLER

Honorary Life-Vice President RDA. Crown Equerry from 1961 until his recent retirement. President of numerous Horse & Pony societies and President of the Royal International Horse Show 1993. Also past President of the British Horse Society.

Pheasant Breasts
with ginger creme fraiche & yoghurt

(Serves 4 – 6 people)

2	skinned pheasants
1 tblsp	oil
1 large	onion, finely chopped
6 cloves	garlic (or to taste) finely chopped
1 tblsp	flour
1 tsp	ground ginger
4floz (110ml)	Greek yoghurt
4floz (110ml)	creme fraiche
4oz (110g)	green seedless grapes
salt and freshly ground black pepper	

The day before – joint the pheasants so you have 4 breasts, 4 legs. Wrap the breasts and refrigerate until needed. (The carcases make good stock, and for the legs find a good recipe for coq-au-vin, being generous with the bacon and shallots as of course pheasant legs are not as meaty as chicken legs.)

The next day, pre-heat oven to 350°F, 180°C, Gas 4.

In a fireproof casserole sauté the onion and garlic. Remove from the pan. Brown the pheasant breasts on both sides. Remove from the pan.

Add the flour and ginger to make a roux, then add pheasant stock until sauce becomes roughly the consistency of double cream. There should be enough to cover the breasts. Return the breasts and onion mixture to the casserole, with the sauce. Cover and cook in oven for about 40 minutes.

Remove breasts from the pan and place in an ovenproof serving dish. Leave the sauce in the casserole. Add the creme fraiche and yoghurt, gently reheat to just below boiling. Adjust for seasoning and pour the sauce over the pheasant breasts. Garnish with grapes.

ZARA CAMPBELL-HARRIS, WYFOLD GROUP, SOUTH REGION

Venison
cooked in beer

(Serves 6 – 8 people)

2lbs (900g)	**haunch of venison (roe)**
1 tblsp	**cooking oil**
1oz (25g)	**butter**
8oz (225g)	**onions, sliced**
1lb (450g)	**root vegetables, parsnip, carrot roughly chopped (or pumpkin)**
1/2 pt (275ml)	**light beer**
1 tblsp	**apple or red currant jelly**
1/4 pt (150ml)	**double cream (optional)**
salt and freshly ground black pepper	

Pre-heat oven to 300°F, 150°C, Gas 2

In a fireproof casserole melt the butter with the oil, sauté the sliced onion. Brown the joint on all sides in the casserole then add the root vegetables. Pour the beer over the meat and vegetables, add the jelly. Cover the casserole and place in the oven to cook for 1 1/2 – 2 hours, depending on the age of the meat.

Remove the meat from the dish and slice off the bone. Arrange in a serving dish. Reduce the sauce until thickish, stir in the cream at this stage if you wish it, re-heat and pour the sauce over the meat, or serve separately.

NICKY STENT, ITCHEN VALLEY GROUP, SOUTH REGION

Robbins Bush Rabbit

(Serves 4 people)

1	whole rabbit
1 tblsp	cooking oil
For the stuffing	
8oz (225g)	stale loaf
1 medium	onion, chopped
2 tblsp	parsley, chopped
1 tblsp	sage, chopped OR
1 tsp	dried sage
2 rashers	bacon, fried and finely chopped
1	egg, beaten
salt and freshly ground black pepper	

Pre-heat oven to 350°F, 180°C, Gas 4

Soak the bread in cold water. When completely saturated squeeze it out as dry as possible with your hands. Place in a large bowl and fluff up. Add all the other ingredients and bind with the beaten egg.

Stuff the cavity of the rabbit with the mixture.

Brush the rabbit all over with oil. Wrap in aluminium foil and roast in the oven for about 1 hour.

PAULINE BLACK, NEW FOREST DRIVING GROUP, SOUTH REGION

The group joined the RDA in 1984. They have 6 ponies, 22 disabled drivers and 28 helpers. For the past ten years they have been running holidays for other groups and have a beautiful area in which to vary their drives.

Rabbit with Apricot

in a Cabernet Sauce

(Serves 4 people)

1	whole rabbit
1/2 pt (275ml)	Cabernet Sauvignon
2floz (55ml)	red wine vinegar
2 cloves	garlic unpeeled
5oz (150g)	dried apricots
coarse salt and freshly ground black pepper	
3 tblsp	peanut oil
4oz (110g)	butter
1/2 pt (275ml)	rabbit stock

Bone the rabbit, cut the meat into cubes and marinate for 12 hours in the wine, vinegar and garlic. Cover to avoid it drying out.

Soak the apricots in cold water for 1 hour and then drain.

Drain the rabbit, reserve the marinade. Pat it dry and season with the salt and pepper.

In a heavy fireproof casserole, heat the oil and the butter. Add the cubed rabbit and brown the meat. Add the garlic from the marinade, the reserved marinade, the apricots and the rabbit stock.

Cut wax or parchment paper to fit the casserole, butter the underside and place it over the rabbit, cover the casserole and simmer for 20-30 minutes. Retrieve the cloves of garlic, peel and crush them. Remove the rabbit and apricots and keep warm. Stir the crushed garlic into the sauce and serve the rabbit and apricots with the sauce over the top.

Serve with carrots, asparagus and boiled potatoes.

Rabbit Stock

- rabbit bones
- 1oz (25g) dripping or butter/oil
- 1/2 lb (225g) carrots
- 1/2 lb (225g) celery
- 1 onion
- 1pt (570ml) water
- salt and peppercorns

Using the bones from the rabbit, fry them in the dripping (or butter with oil) until brown, cover with water, add the sliced celery, onion, carrot, add a little salt and a few peppercorns. Simmer for at least an hour then strain.

TYNE & WEAR GROUP, NORTH REGION

From Miss Vanda H Salmon

Game Pie

"This recipe was given to my grandmother by the wife of a Cumberland gamekeeper in about 1898. It is delicious – but very rich! Served hot, accompanied by slices of marrow (or spinach) cooked and then lightly fried in butter. I think it is really best served cold with salad."

(Serves at least 4 people)

cold (cooked) game, wild duck, goose, venison, etc.	
8oz (225g)	sausage meat, well seasoned
6 rashers	bacon
2	eggs, hard boiled
2	tomatoes, ripe and skinned
2	Spanish onions, thinly sliced
2 tsp	horseradish (freshly made if possible)
Herbs, salt and freshly ground black pepper to taste	

Pre-heat oven to 375°F, 190°C, Gas 5

Line a large pie dish with short crust pastry.

Cook the sausage meat and onions, mix together. Thinly slice the onions and hard boiled eggs.

Carve off the bone, in thin slices any game in the larder.

Line the pastry case with slices of game, followed by a layer of the sausage meat and onion, a layer of bacon, a layer of sliced tomato and hard boiled egg and a sprinkling of herbs, salt and pepper. Follow with another layer of game and a layer of bacon, this time with a few dabs of horseradish on it. In this way fill up the pie dish.

Cover the top with a pastry lid, brush with egg and put into the oven to cook the pastry.

VANDA H SALMON

Honorary Life Vice-President RDA. Has led a very full life in spite of being severely disabled in a riding accident. She was secretary to Professor Geoffrey Harrison who founded the Bird Sanctuary near Bradbourne, and also worked in the House of Lords. She now lives in Fife, involved in many local organsiations and breeds Welsh Ponies. She also bred King Charles spaniels.

Fenland Pie

Any combination of game can be used:- Pigeon breasts, Pheasant, Partridge, Rabbit, Hare, Venison, etc.

(Serves 4 – 6 people)

2lbs (900g)	mixed game (uncooked)
8oz (225g)	smoked back bacon (or to taste)
1 or 2	eggs, hard boiled
8oz (225g)	onion, thinly sliced
salt and freshly ground black pepper	
8oz (225g)	puff (or suet) pastry
1/2 pt (275ml)	game stock
salt and freshly ground black pepper	

Pre-heat oven to 400°F, 200°C, Gas 6

Cut the meat into thin slices, chop the eggs and the bacon. Put all the prepared game into a lightly greased 2 pint (1 ltr) pie dish, in layers, seasoning each layer and placing the egg and bacon between layers. Pour over the stock to three-quarter fill the dish.

Cover with pastry, make an air hole, brush over with milk and bake until the pastry has risen and started to brown (about 1/2 an hour). Reduce the oven temperature and cook for about a further hour.

If the pie is to be eaten hot the remaining stock can be served as additional gravy or added to the pie.

If you wish to eat the pie cold the stock should be added at the end of cooking and left to set to jelly.

ANGELA WILSON, HEREWARD GROUP, EAST REGION

Betty's Sauce

For turning cold pheasant or chicken into a delicious, hot dinner party dish.

(Serves 4 people)

1/2 pt (150ml)	double cream
1 tblsp	Worcester Sauce
1 tblsp	fruit chutney
1/2 tsp	french mustard

Preheat oven to 375°F, 190°C, Gas 5

Lightly whip the cream and stir in the other ingredients. Place the carved cold pheasant or chicken in a shallow ovenproof dish, spoon over the sauce and refrigerate for a few hours. Heat thoroughly in the oven.

THE HON MRS NICHOLAS ASSHETON, KNIGHTSBRIDGE GROUP, GREATER LONDON

The group started in May 1973 – they have planted a Horse Chestnut tree to celebrate their 20th Anniversary. The helpers (5 of the originals still help) are constantly pleased and surprised at the improvement achieved by even the most disabled of their riders.

Plum Sauce

for Chops, Steak and Venison

2 tblsp	Worcester Sauce
2 tblsp	red plum jam
2 tblsp	brown sugar
1 tblsp	cornflour water
optional	
	onions, small red pepper, mushrooms, all lightly fried first

Heat all the ingredients in a saucepan, using the slaked cornflour to thicken.

SHEELAGH BENHAM, LUSBURN GROUP.

suppers & light meals

From Mrs Peter Robeson

Avocado Ring

Wine Recommendation

This creamy dish requires a full-bodied white wine to cut through the richness. Treat yourself to Wakefield Clare Valley White from Australia.

For the ring	
3 medium	avocados (with the flesh scooped out)
8oz (225g)	Philadelphia Cheese
2 tblsp	fromage fraiche
2 tblsp	natural yoghurt
4-5 tblsp	chicken stock
1 sachet (10g)	aspic jelly
Filling for the centre	
1lb (450g)	peeled prawns
2 tblsp	fromage fraiche
2 tblsp	natural yoghurt
1 tblsp	mayonnaise
chopped gherkins and tomato puree to taste	

Lightly oil a tin ring mould.

For the ring process all the ring ingredients (except the aspic jelly).

Dissolve the aspic jelly in 4 tablespoons of boiling water and let it cool. Then pour the cooled aspic jelly into the mixture and stir. Spoon mixture into the ring mould, smooth, cover and refrigerate until set.

For the filling mix the ingredients together and put into the centre of the unmoulded avocado ring.

MRS PETER ROBESON

Vice President RDA. A very successful young show jumper, now recognised as a very talented garderner and dendrologist.

From Mrs W Buchanan

Asparagus Mousse

"A well tried recipe, quick easy and popular."

(Serves 8 people)

4 tsp	**gelatine**
1/2 pt (275ml)	**chicken stock**
1 x 10oz tin	**asparagus spears OR you could use avocado**
1/2 pt (275ml)	**mayonnaise**
2	**egg whites**

Soak the gelatine in the stock in a pan, then heat to dissolve the gelatine, allow to cool.

Drain the liquid from the asparagus and reserve a few tips for decoration. Blend the remaining asparagus with the mayonnaise. Whip the egg whites until they are stiff. Stir the cooled gelatine/stock into the asparagus mixture. Add a little egg white, stir, then fold in the rest.

Spoon into a mould or individual ramekin dishes. Allow to set. Decorate before serving.

MRS W BUCHANAN

Honorary Life Vice-President RDA. Chairman of Greater London Region 1975-82. Memeber of RDA Council 1984-90.

Fastest Pizza in the West

When we have groups of hungry children crowding the kitchen after riding it is easy for each to make his/her own base. A variety of toppings are available in bowls on the table – bacon pieces, chopped ham, mushrooms, onions, tuna, chicken pieces, etc. Each child then creates his/her favourite topping mix. A very satisfying end to a happy morning and the smell is wonderful! Made and enjoyed within thirty minutes.

Makes 4 pizza

For the basic recipe

12oz (350g)	**self raising flour**
1 tsp	**salt**
4oz (110g)	**butter**
1/2 pt (275ml)	**milk**

For the topping

14oz (400g)	**can tomatoes, chopped**
1 tsp	**mixed herbs**
salt and freshly ground black pepper	
2oz (50g)	**cheese, grated**

Pre-heat oven to 425°F, 220°C, Gas 7

Rub the fat into the flour and salt. Add the milk and make into a dough. Knead the dough for 2 minutes. Cut into four and flatten into a pizza shape. Place on a greased baking tray.

Drain the tomatoes (save the juice for stews, etc.) and mix with herbs, salt and pepper and spread over the pizza bases. Next spread with your choice of topping, sprinkle cheese on top and bake in the oven for 20 minutes until golden.

Eat and enjoy.

SUSAN ELKS & JILLY WOOKEY, ROCKLEY GROUP, MID WEST REGION

The group started in 1984 and caters almost exclusively for children with emotional and behavioural difficulties. They ride once a week during term time and in the summer there are sponsored whole day rides up onto the Marlborough Downs. A gymkhana is held at the end of the winter term in the indoor school. The small band of dedicated helpers are quite special themselves – for these demanding children with their challenging behaviour need a lot of sensitive handling.

From Jenny Pitman

Quiche

6oz (175g)	plain flour
3oz (75g)	lard
3oz (75g)	margarine
4oz (110g)	bacon, chopped
2	tomatoes, sliced
1/2	green pepper, chopped
2oz (50g)	onions, chopped
2oz (50g)	mushrooms, sliced
4oz (110g)	cheese, grated
1/4 pt (150g)	milk
2	eggs
herbs	
salt and freshly ground black pepper	

Pre-heat oven to 400°F, 200°C, Gas 6

Rub fat into flour with a little salt and pepper until fine breadcrumbs. Add a little water to make a dough. Roll out and line a flan dish. Bake for 10 minutes.

Put bacon, tomatoes, peppers, onions and mushrooms into a bowl and microwave until just tender. Add herbs, salt and pepper.

Put into a baked flan case and cover with cheese. Pour over the beaten egg and milk. Bake in oven for 30-40 minutes or until top is golden and firm to touch.

Leave to stand for an hour and serve hot or cold.

MRS JENNY PITMAN

The most successful female National Hunt trainer of all time, Jenny Pitman has trained winners of many of the great races including Corbiere for the Grand National in 1983 and Garrison Savannah for the 1991 Gold Cup.

Cabbage Sausage Parcels

(Serves 4 – 6 people)

1	cabbage, savoy type
1-2	sausages per person depending on size of sausage
1/2 pt (275ml)	cheese sauce
4oz (110g)	cheese grated
2	Weetabix, or breadcrumbs

Pre-heat oven to 375°F, 190°C, Gas 5

Blanche a whole outside cabbage leaf per each sausage. Refresh in cold water. Part cook the sausage and wrap each in a cabbage leaf. Place in a greased ovenproof dish.

Make the cheese sauce, enough to cover the sausages. Sprinkle with the grated cheese and crunched up Weetabix (or breadcrumbs).

Cook in the oven until cooked through and brown, for 20-30 minutes.

NICKY STENT, ITCHEN VALLEY GROUP, SOUTH REGION

Special Burgers

(Serves 4 people)

1	egg, beaten
2 tblsp	natural yoghurt
6	spring onions
2 tblsp	french mustard
2 cloves	garlic
1lb (450g)	minced beef (finely minced)
2 tblsp	fresh breadcrumbs
salt and freshly ground black pepper	

Trim and finely chop the spring onions. Peel and finely chop the garlic.

Mix the beaten egg and yoghurt together in a mixing bowl, stir in the mustard, garlic, onions and breadcrumbs. Season.

Mix in the meat. Shape the mixture into four patties, about an inch thick.

Chill for about an hour. Brush with a little oil or barbecue sauce and grill for about eight minutes on each side. Serve in split baps toasted over the barbecue.

HITTISLEIGH GROUP, SOUTH WEST REGION

This recipe has been used very successfully at barbecues held by the group. The burgers were especially appreciated by Jan Barber who completed a walk from John O'Groats to Lands End in 1993. She stopped at Crediton and before putting her feet up for the night was entertained to a riding display and barbecue.

From Lucinda Green

Bobotie

(Serves 4 – 6 people)

1/2 oz (10g)	butter
2 medium	onions, chopped
1lb (450g)	minced beef or lamb
1 thick slice	white bread, crumbled
2 medium	carrots, grated
1 tblsp	curry powder
1oz (25g)	cashew nuts, chopped
1 tblsp	cider vinegar
1 tblsp	chutney
1 tblsp	apricot jam
1 tblsp	seedless raisins
1 tblsp	sultanas
1 tsp	turmeric
1/2 pt (275ml)	beef stock
1 tblsp	whole blanched almonds
lemon or bay leaves	
1	egg, beaten
2 tblsp	milk
salt and freshly ground black pepper	

Pre-heat oven to 325°F, 170°C, Gas 3

Gently fry the onions in the butter until they are transparent. Increase the heat and add the minced beef, cook until browned. Then add the bread and grated carrots and stir well.

Mix together the curry powder, chopped nuts, vinegar, chutney, jam, raisins, sultanas and turmeric, add to the mince. Stir in the stock and simmer for about 10 minutes, adjust the seasoning. Transfer to an oven-proof dish, adding the almonds and bay leaves onto the top. Cover and bake for 25 minutes.

Beat the egg and milk together, seasoning lightly and pour over the meat. Return to the oven uncovered and bake until the "custard" has set, 8-15 minutes.

Serve with yellow rice, chutney, coconut, chopped tomatoes, bananas, etc.

LUCINDA GREEN M.B.E.

An outstandingly, successful 3 day Event Rider her record includes 6 victories at the Badminton Horse Trials ('73, '76, '77, '79, '83, '84) and victories at Burghley in '77 and '81. She was European Champion in 1975 and '77 and World Champion in 1982.

Ham & Green Pepper in Cheese Sauce

This is very simple, and very tasty.

(Serves 6 people)

12 thin	slices of ham
1 or 2	green peppers (depending on size or taste)
For the Cheese Sauce	
2oz (50g)	butter or margarine
2oz (50g)	plain flour
1pt (570ml)	milk
4oz (110g)	cheddar cheese (or to taste)
Salt and freshly ground black pepper	

Pre-heat oven to 350°F, 180°C, Gas 4

Roll the thin slices of ham and place in a buttered oven proof dish. Seed and slice the peppers and scatter in between the rolls.

Make the cheese sauce and pour over the ham & peppers: season to taste.

Bake for about 30 minutes until the peppers are soft and the top is browned.

HOLTWOOD GROUP, SOUTH WEST REGION

Gran's Wartime Ham and Egg Pie

Still popular 50 years on.

(Serves 4 – 6 people)

1lb (450g)	puff pastry
12oz (350g)	chopped ham/pork
8	eggs
4 tblsp	chopped chives
salt and freshly ground black pepper	

Pre-heat oven to 375°F, 190°C, Gas 5

Line a 10" (25cm) pie dish with a little more than 1/2 the pastry, rolled out thinly. Slice 1/2 the meat over the pastry base, break the eggs – keeping them whole, sprinkle with the chives, season, and then cover with the rest of the meat.

Top with the rest of the pastry, seal the edges. Decorate with pastry leaves. Brush with eggwash. Cut a ventilation slot.

Cook for 35-40 minutes in the oven or on the floor of Aga top oven. Cool.

To be eaten just cold with pickles or sauces.

CENTAUR GROUP, NORTH MIDLANDS REGION

From Lord Oaksey

Favos Gisados

Serves 4 people

1lb (450g)	**smoked gammon**
1 medium	**onion**
1 tblsp	**oil**
$1^1/_2$ lb (700g)	**broad beans, young**
1 glass	**dry white wine**
stock to cover	
Freshly ground black pepper	

Cut the gammon into diced pieces. Chop the onion. Fry the onion with the gammon in a little oil until cooked (but not brown). Add the beans with enough stock and wine to cover, put the lid on and simmer gently until the beans are tender (about 5-7 minutes).

Leave to stand off the heat (still covered) for beans to take up the flavour of the gammon.

Re-heat and season when ready to serve. It may not need salt as gammon is quite salty.

This can be made hours before it is needed.

THE LORD OAKSEY

Honorary Life Vice-President RDA. Well-known presenter of racing on Channel 4 Television. Formerly a very successful amateur rider. Stepped in at the last moment to play the veterinary surgeon in the film *Dead Cert*.

Hock n' Dough

A dish from Wellingborough, Northamptonshire. The town was sometimes called after this dish and the local Wellingborough football team is called "The Dough Boys".

(Serves 4 – 6 people)

8oz (225g)	**plain flour**
4oz (110g)	**shredded suet**
2floz (55ml)	**water**
1 small	**onion, grated**
2 medium	**onions, sliced**
1 tblsp	**fresh sage, chopped OR**
1 tsp	**dried sage**
12oz (350g)	**streaky pork, cut into small pieces**
1/2 pt (275ml)	**chicken stock**
1 1/2 lb (700g)	**potatoes, peeled and medium sliced**
salt and freshly ground black pepper	

Pre-heat oven to 350°F, 180°C, Gas 4

Mix together the flour, suet, a little salt and the grated onion. Add cold water to make a dough, knead gently until smooth.

Roll out to line the sides only of an 8 inch (20cm) cake tin (not loose bottomed!) or a souffle dish, lightly greased.

Layer the meat, onions and potatoes finishing with a layer of potatoes neatly arranged in overlapping circles. Season each layer with the sage, pepper and a little salt. There is no need to use salt if using a stock cube.

Pour in the stock until nearly to the top of the tin.

Bake in the centre of the oven for 1 1/2-1 3/4 hours until golden brown. If it browns too quickly lower the oven a little and place a piece of damp greaseproof/parchment paper over it.

MARY HENDRY, KETTERING AND DISTRICT GROUP, NORTH MIDLANDS REGION

Bacon Savoury

(Serves 4 – 6 people)

1lb (450g)	bacon pieces or streaky, chopped
1lb (450g)	onions, sliced
2 tblsp	butter or oil
1 1/2 lb (700g)	potatoes, raw, sliced
2	red peppers, sliced & de-seeded OR
6	tomatoes, sliced
salt and freshly ground black pepper	

Pre-heat oven to 350°F, 180°C, Gas 4

Soften the sliced onions in the microwave or in a pan with a little butter or oil.

Grease a suitable pie dish or casserole. Layer the potatoes and the rest of the ingredients, season with salt and freshly ground black pepper. Dot with oil or butter, cover and cook in the oven for about one hour. Or in the microwave for approximately 15-30 minutes (depending on power).

Serve with a green salad.

LEATHERHEAD GROUP, SOUTH EAST REGION

Started in the Easter Holidays 1974 by Molly Thorn and Florence Tringham, the group has now progressed to an equestrian centre where they are able to borrow suitable ponies for the session with riders coming from the special unit of Eastwick Infant and Junior County School, Great Bookham, Leatherhead.

Cornish Rawfry

This is an old and tried family recipe. The dish was usually served the day before "pay day" in times past as the less well off people had only these few ingredients left in the larder. It is still eaten today and is good with vinegar sprinkled over the top.

(Serves 4 – 6 people)

1 tblsp	**cooking oil**
1lb (450g)	**potatoes, peeled**
1	**onion, roughly chopped**
1/2	**turnip/swede**
1pt (570ml)	**stock**
3	**rashers bacon**
1 tsp	**cornflour**
salt and freshly ground black pepper	

Heat the oil in a large frying pan. Fry half the chopped onion until nearly crisp. Slice the potatoes so that there is a thin layer covering the onions.

Slice some turnip to cover the potato layer. Season with salt and pepper.

Add another layer of onion, potato and turnip. Repeat until the frying pan is full making the final layer potato.

Reduce the heat and put the bacon rashers on top. Add the stock, then put a lid or tin plate over the pan.

Cook on a low heat for 15 minutes. Then mix the cornflour with a little cold water and add to the pan 5 minutes before serving.

LANJETH GROUP, SOUTH WEST REGION

Bacon Roly-Poly

(Serves 4 people)

8oz (225g)	**self raising flour**
pinch	**salt**
pinch	**pepper**
3oz (75g)	**suet or margarine**
water	
8oz (225g)	**streaky bacon, chopped**
1 small	**onion, chopped**
1 tsp	**mixed herbs (or to taste)**
a little stock or gravy	

Make a dough with the flour, fat, salt, pepper and water. Roll out on a floured surface, into an oblong shape about 1/4" thick (1/2cm).

Sprinkle on the bacon, onion, herbs and a little stock or gravy to moisten. Roll up the dough and seal each end.

Wrap a linen cloth around the roly-poly and tie each end with string (like a cracker). Make sure the cloth allows the dough to expand. Immerse in boiling water for 1 1/2-2 hours.

Serve hot with potatoes and root vegetables.

SHERSTONE GROUP, GREATER LONDON REGION

Creole Jambalaya
with Sausage

(Serves 4 people)

1lb (450g)	smoked sausage
8oz (225g)	tomatoes OR
1 tin	tomatoes
2oz (50g)	butter
1	onion, chopped
1 clove	garlic
1/2	red pepper, sliced
1/2	green pepper, sliced
1 tsp	paprika
1/2 tsp	chilli powder
salt and freshly ground black pepper	

Cut the smoked sausage in 1 inch (2 1/2 cm) cubes and chop the tomatoes.

Fry the onions and garlic until soft in the butter, then add the peppers and cook for 5 minutes. Next add the paprika and chilli and cook for a further minute. Then add the tomatoes with all their juices and continue to cook for another 5 minutes. Finally add the sausage and simmer for 15 minutes. Season to taste.

Serve with boiled rice.

JANE DAVENPORT, SNOWBALL FARM GROUP, SOUTH REGION

A small group based near Burnham, Buckinghamshire have the use of facilities, ponies and tack at the equestrian centre. They hold two classes at their weekly meeting with a total of seven riders. Alison has been riding with the group for thirteen years and has passed both grades I and II and is working towards grade III. "It is a never ending source of pleasure for us to see the benefit and delight that these riders gain from riding and contact with their patient mounts. When Paul experienced his first trot there were giggles of delight and his pleas to "do it again". At moments like that all our efforts are rewarded a hundred fold".

Lasagne

(Serves 4 – 6 people)

1 tblsp	cooking oil
1lb (450g)	minced beef
1 large	onion, chopped
1 clove	garlic, chopped
14oz (440g)	can tomatoes
4oz (110g)	mushrooms, sliced
2 tblsp	tomato puree
1	beef stock cube
salt and freshly ground black pepper	
To make the sauce	
1/2 pt (275ml)	milk
1pkt	cheese sauce
4oz (110g)	cheese, strong cheddar or what you wish
lasagne	

Pre-heat oven to 350°F, 180°C, Gas 4

Heat the oil in a pan, add the chopped onion and garlic, cook for a few minutes. Add the minced beef, tomatoes, sliced mushrooms, tomato puree, stock cube and seasoning. Simmer for about 10 minutes.

Make the cheese sauce.

In an ovenproof dish arrange layers of mince, lasagne and cheese sauce. Top with grated cheese.

Bake in the oven for 30-45 minutes.

GAYNOR TONKS, THE WIRRAL GROUP, NORTH WEST REGION
A rider with the group for 11 years.

Hungry Horseman's Hash

Similar to a stuffing mixture, but more substantial, vegetarians could omit the bacon.

(Serves 4 – 6 people)

6	slices smoked bacon, chopped
4oz (110g)	mushrooms, chopped
1 large	onion, chopped
1 large	carrot, grated
8oz (225g)	bread crumbs
1	egg
1 tsp	dried sage
1 tsp	mixed herbs or chopped fresh herbs
salt and freshly ground black pepper	
1/4 pt (140ml)	stock (if needed)
1	tomato
1 tsp	parsley, chopped

Pre-heat oven to 400°F, 200°C, Gas 6

Fry the bacon, mushrooms and onion. Save 1 slice of bacon for topping. Mix all the ingredients together. Bind with the egg (add a little stock if the mixture is too dry).

Place in a loaf tin or terrine dish. Press the mixture firmly. Chop the reserved rasher of bacon and sprinkle on top. Bake for 30 minutes or until cooked.

Garnish with tomato and chopped parsley. Slice and serve hot with salad or potato as a main course or as an accompaniment to a roast.

Amanda Hanlon age 12, Alice Rutherford age 14, Donna Bolton age 14,
Stewart Bell age 17, Jonathan Allan age 17, Tracy Cockburn age 18.
EDINBURGH AND BORDERS REGION

The pupils have worked very hard to create this recipe. They are all pupils in the Special Unit at The Berwickshire High School, Duns. They thought up the name of the dish themselves and it has proved very popular in group cooking sessions.

Sausage and Tomato Casserole

A tasty dish, makes sausages go a long way!

(Serves 4 – 6 people)

$1^1/_2$ lbs (700g)	**good pork sausages**
2 tblsp	**good dripping or oil**
14oz (400g)	**can tomatoes**
2 large	**onions**
1oz (25g)	**flour**
2	**green peppers, seeded and chopped**
1 tblsp	**Worcester Sauce**
1	**bay leaf**
salt and freshly ground black pepper	
6oz (175g)	**brown breadcrumbs & cheese**

Pre-heat oven to 375°F, 190°C, Gas 5

Bring a large saucepan of water to the boil and blanche the sausages for 10 minutes. Drain and when cool enough to handle, skin and cut into thick slanting slices.

Fry the onion slowly in the dripping or oil until golden. Blend in the flour, add the tomatoes and peppers and bring to the boil. Stirring all the while. Add the Worcester Sauce and the bay leaf. Simmer for about 10 minutes to reduce the sauce and adjust the seasoning.

Place the sausages in an ovenproof casserole. Pour the sauce over. Cover generously with the topping of bread crumbs and cheese, whizzed in the food processor. (Cheddar cheese or Parmesan or anything else that may be going hard on the cheese board!) A selection of herbs, marjoram, parsley, basil, may also be whizzed.

Bake for 30 minutes.

MRS C PIKE, HELPER WITH ALDERSHOT GROUP, SOUTH REGION

Un Poit et des Pais au Fou

(Jersey Bean Jar)

This is a very old traditional Jersey dish, referred to as "bean crock" as it was cooked in a large earthenware type pot, some of which were used for many years being passed on through the family.

Many older Jersey people will remember the beans being prepared at home then taken to the local bakehouse or "parish oven" to be left overnight to cook.

(Serves 6 – 8 people)

4oz (110g)	**butter beans**
4oz (110g)	**broad beans**
4oz (110g)	**large red haricot beans**
4oz (110g)	**small pearl haricot**
4oz (110g)	**brown beans**
2lbs (1kg)	**belly of pork or 2 pigs trotters**
1 dsp	**Bisto (optional)**
salt and freshly ground black pepper	

Pre-heat oven to 300°F, 150°C, Gas 2

Soak the beans overnight, at least 12 hours. Then drain and place in a large pan with meat, cover with water. Add the salt and pepper to taste. Bring to the boil and simmer for 30 minutes.

Pour into a casserole, adding herbs if you wish and bake for at least four hours, adding water when necessary.

In the winter time many local functions and socials offer bean crock as supper. Recipes vary slightly from family to family.

JERSEY GROUP, SOUTH REGION

The group started in the late 60s with a very small group. Now there are seventy riders, both adults and children split into five groups. Lessons take place in school grounds, riding schools and sometimes a hack through quiet country lanes.

Pasta Carbonara

(Serves 4 people)

12oz (350g)	pasta shapes of your choice
1 tblsp	extra virgin olive oil
1 small	onion, chopped
2 cloves	garlic, crushed
2	eggs
1/4 pt (150ml)	double cream
2oz (50g)	parmesan, freshly grated
salt and freshly ground black pepper	
6oz (175g)	cooked ham, cut into thin strips

Cook the pasta shapes. Meanwhile heat the olive oil in a pan and gently fry the onion and garlic.

In a bowl mix 2 eggs, the double cream and the parmesan cheese, season.

Drain the cooked pasta, and return it to the saucepan (but do not put back on the heat). Immediately add the cream and egg mixture, the strips of ham, the onion and garlic. Mix over a gentle heat, do not allow to boil.

Serve garnished with chopped parsley and slices of crusty bread, if you wish.

LYNNE NUGENT, MALVERN HILLS GROUP, WEST MERCIA REGION

From Jimmy Savile, OBE

Single Man's Lunch

1 can of beans, 1 can of soup. Pour into pan.
Heat and eat straight from pan.
(No washing up)

SIR JAMES SAVILE, OBE, KCSG, HD

Vice-President RDA. A strong supporter of the RDA, Jimmy Savile is one of Britain's best known personalities through his TV and radio appearances and his work on behalf of the physically handicapped. He has helped to raise over £12 million to rebuild the National Spinal Injuries Centre.

vegetarian & vegetables

Cheese and Onion Flan

(Serves 4 – 6 people)

8oz (225g)	shortcrust pastry
1	egg
8oz (225g)	cheddar cheese, grated
2 medium	onions, sliced or chopped
1 tblsp	oil
salt and freshly ground black pepper	

Pre-heat oven to 400°F, 200°C, Gas 6
Line a greased 6" (10cm) flan tin/dish with the pastry.
Gently cook the onions in the oil for about 5 minutes or until cooked.
In a bowl, beat the egg, add the grated cheese and onions. Season. Mix well and pour into the flan case.
Use any leftover pastry to make a lattice design.
Bake for 30-40 minutes, until slightly risen and golden.

THE WIRRAL GROUP, NORTH WEST REGION

Cheese Fritters

A family wartime recipe still enjoyed.

(Serves 4 people)

1oz (25g)	butter
1/4 pt (150ml)	water
2oz (50g)	plain flour
2-4oz (50-110g)	cheese, grated
1 or 2	eggs
cayenne pepper and salt	

You need either oil in a pan for shallow frying or a deep fat fryer.

Put butter and water in a small saucepan and bring to the boil. Add the flour and beat until the mixture draws away cleanly from the side of the pan.

Take the pan off the heat, add the cheese, egg and seasoning. Mix thoroughly until smooth then turn onto a plate to cool.

When required drop spoonfuls into hot fat and fry to a golden brown.

HARTFIELD GROUP, SOUTH EAST REGION

The group started in 1977 and has 14 young riders and 20 helpers. The ponies are privately owned and the group have the use of an indoor arena in the winter. In the summer they are able to ride through the woods. Each summer there is a weeks holiday with riding every day enjoyed by riders and helpers.

Derwen Country Crumble

(Serves 4 – 6 people)

For the ratatouille

1	aubergine
1lb (450g)	courgettes
1lb (450g)	tomatoes, skinned and chopped
3 large	onions
1 clove	garlic, crushed
2 tblsp	cooking oil
salt and freshly ground black pepper	
1/2 pt (275g)	cheese sauce

For the topping

8oz (225g)	flour
4oz (110g)	margarine
2oz (50g)	cornflakes, crushed
1 tblsp	dry mustard

Pre-heat oven to 350°F, 180°C, Gas 4

Prepare vegetables by slicing thinly but evenly. Fry gently without browning the onions, garlic and courgettes, for about 5-7 minutes. Add the tomatoes, toss gently and cook for a further 15-20 minutes. Season to taste.

Meanwhile make the cheese sauce (or use a packet mix) to a fairly stiff consistency. Sieve together the flour and mustard, rub in the margarine until the mixture resembles breadcrumbs. Add the cornflakes and mix well.

Place the ratatouille mixture on the base of an ovenproof dish. Top with the cheese sauce and cover with the crumble mixture.

Cook in the oven for about 25 minutes until golden and heated through.

HELEN WRIGHT, CHEF TUTOR, BETTY'S COFFEE SHOP, DERWEN COLLEGE AND WORKSHOP FOR THE DISABLED, WEST MERCIA REGION.

The news from Derwen Group is that some of their riding students have gone on to become trainees with The Derwen Enterprises of which Betty's Coffee Shop is one.

Russian-Style Macaroni

This dish is very good for large parties as the cooking time is not an exact science!

(Serves at least 6 – 8 people)

1½ lbs (700g)	macaroni
2 tblsp	cooking oil
1lb (450g)	cabbage, shredded
8oz (225g)	mushrooms, sliced
1	carrot, chopped
1 tsp	caraway seeds
½ pt (275ml)	sour cream, creme fraiche is rather good
¾ pt (425ml)	cottage cheese
8oz (225g)	cheddar cheese, grated (or a bit more)
1	red onion, thinly sliced
2	spring onions, chopped
1	green pepper, chopped
2 tblsp	dark soy sauce
salt and freshly ground black pepper	

Pre-heat oven to 350°F, 180°C, Gas 4

Cook the macaroni, drain and reserve.

Meanwhile in a large pan, heat the oil and sauté the cabbage, mushrooms, carrot and caraway seeds, for about 5 minutes. Mix with the macaroni and add in all the other ingredients, mix well, adjust seasoning. Spoon into a shallow ovenproof dish. Bake for about 40 minutes or cook for 30 minutes and then heat through when required.

VERONICA CARLISLE, HYDE PARK GROUP, GREATER LONDON REGION

Veronica Carlisle says, "I used this recipe (quantities doubled and made 6 times) to feed 100 (easily) at the 1993 Greater London Annual meeting, and made a handsome profit for the group."

Sussex Potato and Cheese Cakes

(Serves 4 people)

8oz (225g)	**cooked mashed potato**
1/2 oz (10g)	**butter**
2	**shallots, chopped OR**
1 medium	**onion, chopped**
2oz (50g)	**plain flour**
2oz (50g)	**cheese, grated**
1	**egg, beaten**
salt and freshly ground black pepper	

Pre-heat oven to 400°F, 200°C, Gas 6

Melt the butter in a small pan and gently cook the shallots or onion for about 5 minutes.

In a bowl mix all the ingredients together and form into small round cakes. Either cook on a pre-heated griddle or frying pan, or on a baking sheet in the oven for 10-15 minutes.

Serve with poached or fried eggs, and for non-vegetarians, rashers of bacon.

GOODWOOD DRIVING GROUP, SOUTH REGION

The driving group was formed in 1987, and they enjoy great pleasure from driving in the beautiful grounds of Goodwood House every week. The group has achieved much and are indebted to their ponies. Without them driving would be impossible!

Calcannon

This is one of the oldest Irish recipies and gets its name from cal (Kale or cabbage) and ceann thionn (white headed) in Irish.

(Serves 6 – 8 people)

6 large	**potatoes peeled and boiled**
6	**shallots or spring onions, chopped**
1/4 pt (150ml)	**sour cream**
8oz (225g)	**curly kale or leaf cabbage (cooked)**
2oz (50g)	**butter**
1 tblsp	**parsley, chopped**
salt and freshly ground black pepper	

Mash the potatoes finely.

Add the onions to the sour cream, bring to just below boiling. Remove from the heat and allow to infuse for at least 10 minutes.

Chop the cabbage finely and add half of the butter, cook for a few minutes.

Fold all the ingredients together and beat hard. Adjust seasoning.

Make a well in the centre and serve with a knob of butter.

MAUREEN WALSH, ENNISKILLEN GROUP, NORTHERN IRELAND

Skirlie

(Serves 2 – 4 people)

4oz (110g)	**medium oatmeal**
2oz (50g)	**dripping**
1	**onion**
salt and freshly ground black pepper	

Melt the dripping in a heavy bottomed frying pan.

Chop the onion finely and fry very slowly in the dripping until soft. Add the oatmeal and fry slowly, stirring from time to time until the oatmeal is well cooked, crisp and light brown.

Season and serve very hot with mashed potato and mashed turnip or cooked cabbage.

BUCHAN GROUP, GRAMPIAN & HIGHLAND REGION

New Potatoes with mushrooms

(Serves 4 people)

1lb (450g)	**new potatoes**
8oz (225g)	**button mushrooms**
2oz (50g)	**butter**
4 tblsp	**double cream**
salt and freshly ground black pepper	
1 tblsp	**chopped parsley (optional)**

Wash the new potatoes. “Scrape if you want to, I always leave mine in their skins”. Boil in salted water until just tender. Drain and keep warm.

Meanwhile wash and trim the mushrooms. Melt the butter in a pan over a low heat, then add the mushrooms and turn them in the butter, increasing the heat. Season.

When the mushrooms give up their juice add cooked (thickly sliced) potatoes, and continue to cook until there is very little liquid left.

Add the cream, bring to the boil, serve sprinkled with parsley if you wish.

ANNETTE HARDY, HELPER WITH STRATFORD UPON AVON GROUP, WEST MERCIA

Braised Red Cabbage

(Serves 4 – 6 people)

1lb (450g)	red cabbage, finely shredded
8oz (225g)	onions, finely chopped
8oz (225g)	cooking apple, finely chopped
1 1/2 tbslp	wine vinegar
1 1/2 tbslp	brown sugar
1 clove	garlic, finely chopped
1/4 tsp	nutmeg
1/4 tsp	cinnamon
4	cloves
salt and freshly ground black pepper	
1/2 oz (10g)	butter

Pre-heat oven to 275°F, 140°C, Gas 1

In a large casserole layer the cabbage, onion and apple. Sprinkle the garlic, spices, sugar, salt and pepper between each layer.

Pour the vinegar over and top with the butter.

Cook for 2-2 1/2 hours, stirring once or twice.

This reheats very well.

WENLO GROUP, NORTH MIDLANDS REGION

Rosti

(Serves 4 – 6 people)

1lb (450g)	potatoes
2	onions
2oz (50g)	melted butter
4oz (110g)	cheddar cheese
	cayenne
salt and freshly ground black pepper	
1 tblsp	oil

Pre-heat oven to 400°F, 200°C, Gas 6

Grate everything. Add seasoning to taste. Put a tin in the oven with the oil in it and when hot, spoon the mixture in and cook for 1 hour.

Serve.

FEN END GROUP, WEST MERCIA

Easy Potato Bake

An unusual and tasty way of serving potatoes.

(Serves 4 people)

$1^1/_2$ lb (700g)	potatoes, peeled and cut in wedges
2	onions, thinly
2 cloves	garlic, crushed
1oz (25g)	butter
4 tblsp	fresh parsley, chopped
pinch	nutmeg
salt and freshly ground black pepper	
For the topping	
2	eggs
$^1/_4$ pt (150ml)	sour cream
2 tblsp	milk
3oz (75g)	cheddar cheese, grated

Pre-heat oven to 375°F, 190°C, Gas 5

Boil the potato wedges in salted water for 5 minutes. Drain well, return to the pan and shake dry over low heat.

Melt the butter and gently fry onions and garlic for about five minutes, without browning. Stir in the parsley.

Layer the potatoes and onion mixture in a shallow ovenproof dish, sprinkle with seasoning and nutmeg.

For the topping – whisk the eggs with the soured cream and milk. Pour over the potatoes and sprinkle with half the cheese.

Cook in the oven for 30 minutes. Sprinkle with the remaining cheese and cook for a further 10-15 minutes until the potatoes are tender and topping is lightly browned. Serve hot.

MOORCROFT SCHOOL GROUP, GREATER LONDON REGION

puddings & desserts

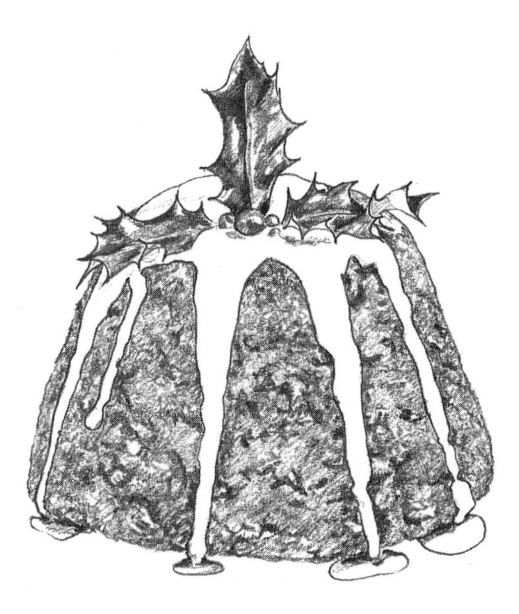

From Lady Jill Freud

Hot Fruit Brûlée

1	orange
1	apple
1	pear
1	banana, sliced
	black grapes
	brown sugar
	spices, optional

Pre-heat oven to 400°F, 200°C, Gas 6

Peel the orange, core the apple and pear, leave skin on and cut into mouth-size pieces. Put with the rest of the fruit into a 1 inch (2½cm) deep ovenproof dish.

Sprinkle with brown sugar to taste, and spices if you want.

Place in oven and cook for 30 minutes. Take out and turn over, sprinkle with a little more sugar and bake for a further 25 minutes.

Serve hot with cream.

LADY JILL FREUD

Vice President RDA. Wife of writer, food critic and ex MP Clement Freud and mother of Emma Freud. Is Artistic Director of her own theatre company in Southwold and for many years ran a holiday camp for the RDA from her home in Walberswick, Suffolk.

Spiced Pears

(Serves 4 – 6 people)

4	eating pears (Comice if you can get them)
4oz (110g)	stoned dates
2 tblsp	lemon juice
2 tblsp	honey
½ tsp	allspice
2 tblsp	water

Pre-heat oven to 300°F, 150°C, Gas 2

Peel, halve and core pears. Push 2 pieces of dates into the core cavity and then lay the pears, cut side down in an oven proof dish. Dribble over the lemon juice and then honey. Sprinkle with allspice. Gently pour in the water around the pears.

Cover with parchment paper and lid (or foil if the dish does not have a lid) and bake in oven until tender but not too soft, for approximately 30 minutes.

Serve hot or warm with vanilla yoghurt.

HANFORD GROUP, SOUTH WEST REGION

From Dr James G Sommerville

Poached Peaches

4	ripe peaches
8	cloves
1oz (25g)	butter
3 1/2 oz (100g)	caster sugar
2floz (55ml)	water
1/2	lemon, the zest

Pre-heat oven to 325°F, 170°C, Gas 3

Put the peaches in a basin and cover with boiling water. Count to approximately 15 by which time they should skin easily.

Stick cloves into each skinned peach and a good knob of butter in the top and place them in a casserole.

Dissolve the sugar in the measured water by heating gently, bring to boiling point and then pour it over the peaches. Sprinkle each peach with a little zest of lemon, cover and bake for 30 minutes. Serve hot or cold.

DR JAMES G SOMMERVILLE, MD, FRCP.

Honorary Life Vice-President RDA. Served on the Council from 1969-73 and was one of the first members of the medical profession to advocate riding for the disabled as a beneficial activity. Particularly interested in the rehabilitation of adults who have suffered serious illness or bad accidents and played a part in the making of the film "The Right to Choose" in 1977.

Baked Rhubarb & Banana Compote

1lb (450g)	young rhubarb
4oz (110g)	caster sugar
1/2	orange, the juice
2	bananas

Pre-heat oven to 350°F, 180°C, Gas 4

Trim, wash and cut rhubarb into 1 inch (2 1/2cm) lengths. Place in a casserole dish with sugar and strained juice of orange. Bake for about 30 minutes or until tender.

Peel and slice the bananas, divide equally among four serving dishes. Spoon over the rhubarb and juice while still hot.

Serve warm or chilled with cream.

MARY HOPKINS, OSWESTRY GROUP, WEST MERCIA REGION

From Virginia Elliot

Mango Cream

(Serves 4 – 6 people)

1 x 14oz (400g) tin	mango
1/2 pt (275ml)	whipping cream
	a little grated nutmeg

Whip the cream until thick. Drain the mangoes through a sieve, and lightly mash, reserving the juice.

Fold together the cream and mangoes, and as much of the reserved juice as is possible.

Spoon into bowls or glasses and grate a little nutmeg over the top.

MRS VIRGINIA ELLIOT M.B.E.

Vice President RDA - as Virginia Leng, she was one of Britain's best known Event riders from the time she won the European Junior Championship in 1973 through to her four Olympic medals from the Games of 1984 & '88 - two Team Silver Medals and two Individual Bronze Medals.

Rommi's Bananas

(Serves 4 – 6 people)

3	bananas
2 tblsp	Rum or Madeira
4oz (110g)	caster sugar
juice of 1	orange
juice of 1	lemon
1/2 pt (275ml)	double cream
1 tblsp	toasted almond flakes

Process/blend the bananas, Rum or Madeira, sugar and juices. Put in a saucepan and bring to the boil, stir well to ensure the sugar is dissolved. Remove from the heat and chill for at least 3 hours.

Whip the cream and fold into the banana mixture. Spoon into individual bowls or one large bowl, chill for a further 3 hours if possible, and top with toasted almond flakes before serving.

LADY GUERNSEY, FEN END GROUP, WEST MERCIA REGION

From Mrs Jane Holderness-Roddam

Pups Pud

(Serves 4 people)

8oz (225g)	Philadelphia cream cheese
1/2 pt (275ml)	natural yoghurt
1/2 pt (275ml)	double cream
generous sprinkling of soft brown sugar	

Whip the cream until fairly thick. Blend together the cheese, yoghurt and cream until smooth.
Pour into a dish and sprinkle generously with sugar.
Chill, best served within 12 hours.

JANE HOLDERNESS-RODDAM

Vice President RDA. A well-known event rider and lady-in-waiting to the Princess Royal.

Apple Doo-Dah

(Serves 6 – 8 people)

3lb (1kg 350g)	cooking apples
4oz (110g)	raisins
8oz (225g)	stoned dates
1/4 tsp	cinnamon
1/4 tsp	allspice
1/2 pt (275ml)	orange juice (and sherry- optional)
4oz (110g)	soft dark brown sugar

Pre-heat oven to 375°F, 190°C, Gas 5

Peel, core and slice the cooking apples. Place in the ovenproof dish together with the raisins, dates and spices. Pour the orange juice (and sherry) over and top with the brown sugar. Cover and cook for about 30 minutes until the apples are soft.

Serve hot or cold with cream.

WINDMILL GROUP, EAST REGION

A small group meeting once a week using four horses for up to eight children who have severe learning difficulties. They are fortunate to have a regular volunteer physiotherapist amonst the helpers. They have an anuual summer picnic and of course various fundraising events.

Chestnut Meringue Gateau

Ideal for a sweet, a teatime cake or just spoiling yourself over Christmas.

(Serves 6 – 8 people)

6	**egg whites**
12oz (350g)	**caster sugar**
1pt (570ml)	**double cream**
1 medium tin	**chestnut puree**
To decorate	
4oz (110g)	**fresh chestnuts - cooked, roasted**

Pre-heat the oven to 200°F, 100°C, Gas 1/4

Line 3, 7 inch (18cm) sandwich tins, lightly oiled, with the base lined with oiled parchment paper.

Whisk the egg whites in a bowl until they are stiff. Then whisk in the sugar, a little at a time. Divide the mixture equally between the three tins and smooth them out. Bake the meringues for about 1 hour.

Leave to cool, then loosen the edges, turn out onto wire racks and remove the base paper.

Whip cream until it is softly stiff (i.e. not too stiff) then using only half (reserve the other half for decorating the top) fold in the chestnut puree. Sandwich the three layers together with the cream/chestnut puree.

Decorate the top with whole (or halved) roasted chestnuts and swirls of cream. Fill the gateau four hours before eating and it will be easier to serve.

Note – hazelnuts make an excellent substitute for chestnuts. About 6-8oz (200g).

BERYL SAINSBURY, STRATFORD UPON AVON GROUP, WEST MERCIA REGION

Chocolate Raspberry Meringues

(Serves 6 people)

For the meringue

4oz (110g)	**plain chocolate**
4	**egg whites**
8oz (225g)	**caster sugar**

For the filling & sauce

1/2 pt (275ml)	**double cream**
1lb (450g)	**raspberries**
	a little icing sugar

Pre-heat oven to 200°F, 100°C, Gas 1/4

Line 2 baking sheets with non-stick parchment paper.

For the Meringues finely grate the chocolate. Whisk the egg whites until stiff. Whisk in half the sugar until shiny and stiff. Fold in the remaining sugar and the chocolate.

Shape into meringues of the required size (30 small, or less if they are larger) and bake for 2 hours.

Cool and store in airtight containers for up to 3 weeks.

For the filling and sauce whip the cream with icing sugar to taste. Fold in a few raspberries and sandwich the meringues.

Rub the remaining raspberries through a sieve to make a coulis and pour around the meringues to serve.

HARTFIELD GROUP, SOUTH EAST REGION

Strawberry Charlotte

A delicious sweet for a dinner party or special occasion. If you take this recipe step by step it is simpler than it looks.

(Serves 4 – 6 people)

For the sponge

4	egg yolks
2oz (50g)	caster sugar
3	egg whites
2½ oz (60g)	plain flour
2 tblsp	strawberry jam
1 tblsp	vodka (optional)

For the Charlotte

8oz (225g)	fresh strawberries (wild if possible)
1oz (25g)	caster sugar
1 tsp	vanilla essence
1 tblsp	brandy
4 egg	yolks
4oz (110g)	caster sugar
½ pt (275g)	milk
1	vanilla pod or drop essence
1 pkt (10g)	gelatine (or 4 leaves)
½ pt (275ml)	double cream
1oz (25g)	caster sugar
2 tblsp	apricot jam (for glaze)

Pre-heat oven to 350°F, 180°C, Gas 4
Line an 8"-9" (22cm) baking tray with greaseproof/ parchment paper.

In one bowl using an electric whisk beat the egg yolks and a tablespoon of the caster sugar, until the mixture is thick and creamy. In a separate bowl whisk the egg whites, adding the remaining sugar gradually, until it is stiff. Fold egg yolk mixture into the meringue mixture and finally fold in the sifted flour.

Spread the sponge mixture into a baking tray and bake for 10-15 minutes. Turn the sponge out onto a damp cloth.

Tip – to remove the greaseproof paper with ease dampen the paper with another cloth, thus causing a little steam which will help with the removal of the greaseproof.

Heat the strawberry jam with the vodka and pass through a sieve. Spread over the sponge. Roll the sponge up tightly, like a swiss roll and leave to cool and set. Take a 2pt (1ltr) pudding mould, lightly greased with butter, and line it with 1/4" (1cm) thick slices of the swiss roll, try to place each piece as closely as possible.

For the Charlotte

Place the strawberries, sugar, vanilla essence and brandy in a bowl, toss lightly and leave to marinate for a few minutes.

Meanwhile bring the milk, together with the split vanilla pod (or essence) to the boil, remove from heat and allow to infuse.

Cream together the egg yolks and sugar, gradually add the milk, stirring all the time with a wooden spoon, return to a gentle heat and keep on stirring until the custard coats the back of the spoon. Dissolve the gelatine in approximately 2 tablespoons of water, and add to the warm custard. Pour the custard into the bowl, and place over some ice until it starts to thicken.

Whip the cream and sugar until it is stiff. Finally fold all the ingredients together, (strawberries, custard and cream) and spoon into the lined pudding basin mould. If there is any of the sponge left over place this on top of the mixture.

Leave to set for 2-3 hours. Turn out carefully onto a serving dish. Glaze with warmed sieved apricot jam.

Serve with chocolate dipped strawberries and chocolate sauce.

NICKY BELL, MARKINGTON GROUP, YORKSHIRE & CLEVELAND REGION

Having battled with rheumatoid arthritis since 1986 Nicky was finally forced to retire from her active life as a patisseure. She has discovered the RDA and says how wonderful riding and the group has been to her.

From Mr W J McBride, MBE

Tropical Trifle

(Serves 6 people)

1	ginger cake
2	ripe mangoes (or tin)
8oz (225g)	fresh pineapple (or tin)
2	bananas
2 tblsp	ginger syrup (from jar of preserved stem ginger)
6 tblsp	rum
1pt (570ml)	custard
1/2 pt (275ml)	double cream
1 tblsp	lemon juice
2 tblsp	icing sugar
3 tblsp	desiccated coconut, toasted
1-2 pieces	stem ginger

Cut the cake and arrange in the bottom of a large serving bowl.

Put the mangoes, pineapple, bananas, all peeled and chopped, into the bowl. Mix the ginger syrup and 4 tablespoons of rum together and pour over the fruit cake.

Pour the custard over the fruit. Chill. Meanwhile whip the cream, add 2 tablespoons rum, the lemon juice and icing sugar. Smooth over the custard.

Decorate with coconut and pieces of ginger.

W J McBRIDE, M.B.E.

Vice President RDA. "Willie John" McBride is one of the legends of Irish and British Lions rugby and a long standing supporter of the RDA.

From Mark Todd

Chocolate Fudge Pudding

For the pudding	
3oz (175g)	margarine
2oz (50g)	self raising flour
1oz (25g)	chocolate powder
3oz (75g)	caster sugar
1	egg
For the sauce	
2oz (50g)	brown sugar
1/2 oz (10g)	cocoa powder
1 1/2 oz (40g)	walnuts
1/2 pt (275ml)	hot black coffee
2oz (50g)	caster sugar
icing sugar to dredge	

Pre-heat oven to 325°F, 170°C, Gas 3

Sieve together the flour and chocolate powder into a bowl. Add the rest of the pudding ingredients and beat together until well mixed. Spoon into a greased 2pt (1ltr)pie dish.

Sprinkle with the sugar, cocoa and nut mixture. Carefully pour over the coffee.

Bake for 50-60 minutes.

Dust with icing sugar.

Serve hot with cream.

MARK TODD

An outstanding horseman, representing New Zealand in three consecutive Olympic Games (1984/88/92) and doubling up in both 3 day eventing and show jumping in 88 and 92. Twice Olympic Gold Medal winner in 3 day eventing in 84 and 88.

From Miss Felicity Goodey

Yorkshire Sticky Toffee Pudding

"This recipe was given to me by a lady in Yorkshire where we were out walking one weekend. It is absolutely wicked and should be eaten only after strenuous exercise!! It is too rich to eat alone. It should be served with ice-cream – lots!!"

For the pudding	
6oz (175g)	dates
1/2 pt (275ml)	water
2oz (50g)	butter
6oz (175g)	sugar
1	egg
1/2 tsp	bicarbonate of soda
8oz (225g)	self raising flour
1 tsp	vanilla essence
For the topping	
1/2 pt	double cream
10oz (275g)	brown sugar
6oz (175g)	butter

Pre-heat oven to 325°F, 170°C, Gas 3

Cook the dates gently and briefly in the water until softened.

Cream the butter and sugar and beat in the egg. Add the rest of the pudding ingredients.

Pour into a greased deep square or round dish.

Bake until firm, about 30-40 minutes. When cooked prick the sponge all over with a skewer.

Cook the sugar and butter together until boiling. Stir in the cream and pour over the sponge. Return to the oven for 10 minutes.

Serve with good vanilla ice-cream.

FELICITY GOODEY

Vice President RDA. Senior presenter for News and Current Affairs with BBC TV and Radio (North). Closely involved with the development and work of the RDA in the North West of England for many years.

From Mrs E Holland-Martin

Bread & Butter Pudding
with a difference

12 slices	malt loaf with raisins
4oz (110g)	butter
$^3/_4$ pt (425ml)	single cream
2oz (55ml)	caster sugar
$^1/_2$	lemon, zest
$^1/_2$	orange, zest
1	egg
2	egg yolks
good grating of nutmeg	
1 tblsp	demerara sugar

Pre-heat oven to 350°F, 180°C, Gas 4

Butter each slice of bread, cut in half and arrange in a buttered, shallow ovenproof dish.

Beat together the cream, sugar, egg and egg yolks. Add the grated nutmeg and pour over the bread.

Sprinkle the demerara sugar and the zest of the orange and lemon on top and bake in the oven for 20-25 minutes until the pudding gently wobbles when shaken.

MRS E HOLLAND-MARTIN

Honorary Life Vice-President RDA. Judged the Bob Stanley Memorial Competitions for the RDA groups for many years. Introduced the Holland-Martin Award for disabled riders who have made an outstanding contribution to the work of the association.

Luxury Bread & Butter Pudding

This is an excellent way of using up stale bread, white or brown.

(Serves 4 – 6 people)

3oz (75g)	sultanas
2 tblsp	Cointreau or Amaretto
1/2 pt (275g)	milk
1	vanilla pod
2oz (50g)	caster sugar
2	eggs
1/4 pt (150ml)	cream
4 tblsp	apricot jam
8	thin slices white bread (generously buttered)
4oz (110g)	butter
2oz (50g)	flaked almonds, toasted

Pre-heat oven to 350°F, 180°C, Gas 4

Soak the sultanas in Cointreau or Amaretto overnight or for 6 hours.

Put milk, vanilla pod (or 1/4 tsp vanilla essence) and sugar into a saucepan, bring to the boil, then allow to cool. Beat the eggs and cream together, gradually blending in the milk mixture. Butter the bread and sandwich together with 1/2 the apricot jam – the butter should be on the outside of the sandwich. Remove the crusts and cut the sandwiches in four diagonal shapes. (Keep the crusts for the bottom of the pudding dish if you wish).

Arrange the diagonal sandwiches in layers in a greased 2pt (1ltr) pudding dish, sprinkling each layer with the soaked sultanas. Gradually pour the cream mixture over the bread, ensuring all the bread is covered. Leave to stand for 30-60 minutes to allow the bread to absorb the liquid.

Place the dish in a bain-marie (a roasting tin with about 2" (5cm) water in it) and bake the pudding for 50-60 minutes until the top is crisp and golden.

Meanwhile press the remaining jam through a sieve into a saucepan. Add 1 tablespoon water and heat gently. When the pudding is removed from the oven, brush the jam over the top and sprinkle with the toasted almond flakes. Dredge lightly with icing sugar.

Serve warm, not hot.

RUTHVEN DRIVING GROUP AT GLENEAGLES
WEST AND CENTRAL SCOTLAND REGION

Almond Eve's Pudding

A traditional family pudding. Good in autumn and winter.

(Serves 4 – 6 people)

1½ lb (700g)	cooking apples
2oz (50g)	granulated sugar
For the sponge	
4oz (110g)	soft butter or margarine
4oz (110g)	caster sugar
2	eggs (beaten)
2oz (50g)	self raising flour
2oz (50g)	ground almonds
a few drops	vanilla essence
2 tblsp	milk
1oz (25g)	flaked almonds
To finish	
1 tblsp	icing sugar

Pre-heat oven to 350°F, 180°C, Gas 4

Peel, quarter, core and slice the apples. Put into a saucepan with the sugar, cover and steam gently until tender. Turn into a greased 2 pt (1ltr) pudding dish.

Meanwhile, **to make the sponge** put the butter, caster sugar, eggs, flour, ground almonds, essence and milk in a bowl and beat together until the mixture is smooth and fluffy. About 4 minutes with an electric whisk.

Spoon the mixture on top of the apples. Sprinkle the flaked almonds on top. Bake for 45-50 minutes, or until risen and golden.

Allow to cool for 5 minutes before dusting with icing sugar. Serve either warm with custard or cold with fresh cream.

Note: This pudding may be varied by using tinned fruit, and/or a plain sponge mixture.

MRS HEATHER SHEARLAW, INVERGARVEN GROUP,
WEST AND CENTRAL SCOTLAND REGION

From Jimmy Hill

Old Fashioned Rice Pudding

(Serves 4 people)

2 tblsp	pudding rice
1 pt (570ml)	milk
1oz (25g)	butter
2 tblsp	sugar
a little double cream (optional)	

Pre-heat oven to 375°F, 190°C, Gas 5

Wash the rice thoroughly and cover the bottom of a greased pudding dish. Add the milk and sugar then dot with the butter. If you want a creamier rice pudding add a little cream to the milk.

Put in the oven until a nice skin starts to appear, then turn the heat down to medium/slow and finish cooking. This can take 1 1/2 hours. The longer the better.

Serve hot with freshly stewed fruit.

JIMMY HILL

Vice-President RDA. Was instrumental in getting RDA accepted as one of the charities to benefit from the Ritz Club Trophy funds – the trophy is presented to the winning jockey at major race meetings. Very well-respected television football commentator and pundit.

Rhubarb and Orange Lattice Tart

(Serves 6 – 8 people)

1lb (450g)	rhubarb
6oz (175g)	caster sugar
1oz (25g)	plain flour
1	egg
1	orange, zest & juice
1	9" (22.5cm) uncooked pastry case (reserve the pastry trimmings)

Pre-heat oven to 325°F, 170°C, Gas 3

Cut the rhubarb into 1 inch (2 1/2cm) pieces. Fill the pastry case.

Blend the sugar, flour, beaten egg and zest of orange in a basin. Make the orange juice up to 1/4pt (150ml) with water. Bring to the boil in a saucepan and pour onto the flour mixture, stirring all the time. Return all the mixture to the saucepan, bring to the boil, stirring all the while, when it has thickened pour over the rhubarb.

Make lattice with the pastry trimmings and bake for 35-40 minutes.

A J DUFFETT, OLD PARK FARNHAM GROUP, SOUTH EAST REGION

Crocus Pudding

This recipe has been passed on by generations of Shropshire farmers' wives. It probably goes back even further. Tansy would have been added (a yellow flowering herb). One reason being it purified the body after the limited diet of Lent, and secondly it was a form of symbolism in remembrance of the bitter herbs eaten by Jews at the Passover.

(Serves 6 – 8 people)

1	**lemon zest and juice**
1pt (570ml)	**milk**
4oz (110g)	**sugar**
2½ tblsp	**cornflour**
10 approx.	**'Boudoir' sponge fingers**
25 approx.	**Ratafia biscuits**
¼ pt (150ml)	**cream**

Make a custard with the lemon zest and juice, milk, sugar and cornflour.

Place the sponge fingers in the bottom of ideally a 7" (18cm) diameter 2" (5cm) depth dish. Soak the sponge fingers with a little of the lemon juice and caster sugar if you wish. This will prevent the biscuits from floating to the top when the custard is added.

Pour the lemon custard over the finger biscuits. Leave to cool and decorate with the Ratafia biscuits and the whipped cream.

DERWEN GROUP, WEST MERCIA REGION

Lemon Mille-Feuille

This is an effective and easy way to make the traditional 'grande' mille-feuille – a thousand layers.

(Serves 6 –8 people)

2 x 1lb (450g)	**frozen puff pastry**
12oz (340g)	**jar lemon curd**
1pt (570g)	**cream**
3oz (75g)	**apricot cream**
optional	
4oz (110g)	**strawberries**
4oz (110g)	**peaches**
4oz (110g)	**raspberries**

Pre-heat oven to 375°F, 190°C, Gas 5

Roll out the puff pastry and cut 3 x 10" (25cm) rounds. Cut out 2 x 6" (15cm) holes. Place the 2 rings and 1 circle on floured baking sheets and cook for about 15 minutes until golden brown.

Strain and heat the apricot jam, and assemble the base and rings using the apricot glaze to stick them together. Glaze the top, outside and inside.

Put aside.

Meanwhile whip the double cream and fold in the lemon curd. Spoon mixture into the centre of the mille-feuille, dredge with icing sugar and serve immediately.

Note – many other fillings may be used such as a selection of fresh seasonal fruits or tinned fruits.

DEBORAH PUXLEY, NEWBURY GROUP, SOUTH REGION

From Captain E Hartley-Edwards

Sticky Toffee Tart

"This is a lazy pud and guaranteed to have more calories to the spoonful than most. Surprisingly, it isn't sickly sweet."

For the pastry	
4oz (110g)	self raising flour
good pinch of salt	
1	egg yolk
2oz (50g)	butter
1 tsp	sugar
water to mix	
For the filling	
1 large tin	condensed milk
3	bananas
good squeeze of lemon, to taste	
1/2 pt (275ml)	double cream, whipped
2oz (50g)	toasted, flaked almonds

Pre-heat oven to 375°F, 190°C, Gas5

To make the pastry mix the ingredients and line the pastry in a 9 inch (22.5cm) flan tin. Bake for 15 minutes. Alternatively be lazy and buy a pastry case from your local supermarket.

To make the filling place tin of condensed milk in boiling water for 1 1/2 hours. Make sure the tin is always covered with water.

Cool for 10 minutes then open and spoon contents into the case.

Mash the bananas and add lemon juice to taste, spread over the toffee in the case.

Top with the whipped cream and sprinkle with a liberal coat of flaked almonds toasted under the grill.

Serve slightly chilled.

CAPTAIN E HARTLEY-EDWARDS

Vice-President RDA. A well known equestrian journalist and author of equestrian books. A fine horseman, an expert in saddlery and judge of Welsh Cobs and ponies.

Black Bottom Pie

(Serves 6 – 8 people)

1	cooked 9" (22.5cm) pie crust
4oz (110g)	caster sugar
2 tblsp	cornflour
1/2 pt (275ml)	milk
2	egg yolks
1 tsp	powdered gelatine
3 tblsp	water
4oz (110g)	plain dark chocolate, grated
for the meringue	
2	egg whites
pinch	cream of tartar
4oz (110g)	caster sugar
2 tsp (10g)	gelatine
4 tblsp	water
1 oz (25g)	plain dark chocolate, grated
1/2 pt (275g)	double cream

Make custard from the caster sugar, cornflour, milk and egg yolks. (Remove one-third from this mixture at this stage). Dissolve gelatine into the water and add to the remaining two-thirds custard while still hot. Add the grated chocolate into the hot custard and beat well. Pour into the pie shell and smooth over (a flat surface to the pie shell gives a better final look).

Make the meringue from the egg whites, cream of tartar and caster sugar. Dissolve the gelatine in the water and add to the meringue while still whisking. Fold into the remaining one-third custard mixture and pour onto the chocolate custard in the pie crust. Leave to set and decorate with grated chocolate and piped cream.

Note – optional extras, add brandy to taste to the chocolate custard or white rum to taste to the white custard. It is RATHER nice!

SUSAN DUDLEY-SMITH, REGIONAL DRIVING REPRESENTATIVE, HUMBERSIDE AND SOUTH YORKSHIRE REGION

Duke of Cambridge Pie

(Serves 4 – 6 people)

1 x 9" (22.5cm) pie crust - cooked or partly cooked

3oz (75g)	**butter**
3oz (75g)	**caster sugar**
4oz (110g)	**raisins**
2oz (75g)	**glace cherries, chopped**
2	**egg yolks**
1 tblsp	**brandy.**

Pre-heat oven to 350°F, 180°C, Gas 4

Put the raisins into a saucepan, cover with water, bring to the boil. Remove from the heat and leave to cool and plump for 5 minutes. Drain.

Melt the butter and sugar over a low heat, add to the beaten egg yolks and brandy, stirring all the time to prevent it curdling. Mix the raisins and chopped glace cherries, and pour the mixture into the pie crust.

Bake for about 40 minutes.

DAN COOPER, WOOKEY HOLE AND WELLS GROUP, SOUTH WEST REGION

Norfolk Syrup Tart

(Serves 6 – 8 people)

1	**baked 8" (20cm) flan case**
8oz (225g)	**golden syrup**
1 large	**lemon, grated zest and juice**
1oz (25g)	**melted butter**
1½ oz (40g)	**plain flour**
2	**egg yolks**
2	**egg whites.**

Pre-heat oven 325°F, 170°C, Gas 3 or baking oven in an Aga

Put syrup into a bowl and blend in the lemon juice and the zest, melted butter and flour. When it is smooth beat in the egg yolks. Whisk the egg white until stiff and then fold into the mixture. Pour into the flan case and bake for about 35 minutes.

Serve cold.

NORWICH AND DISTRICT GROUP, EAST REGION

Lemon Cheesecake

This is a very nice light cheesecake.

(Serves 6 – 8 people)

For the base	
6oz (175g)	digestive biscuits, crushed
2oz (50g)	butter
1oz (25g)	brown sugar
1 tsp	golden syrup
For the topping	
12oz (350g)	cottage cheese/cream cheese
1/4 pt (150ml)	single cream
1/4 pt (150ml)	double or whipping cream
2 large	lemons, juice & zest
4oz (100g)	caster sugar
3	egg yolks
1/2 oz (10g)	gelatine
4 tblsp	water
3	egg whites

To make the base melt the butter, sugar and syrup together, add the crushed biscuits. Mix well, then turn into an 8" (20cm) loose-based cake tin, lined with greaseproof paper. Press firmly into shape, and leave to set.

To make the topping mix together the cheese and single cream, preferably in blender/processor. If not, sieve the cottage cheese until smooth.

Put the egg yolks, caster sugar, juice and zest from the lemons into a bowl. Heat over a pan of hot water, whisking until it is frothy. Allow to cool slightly then gently stir in the cheese and cream mixture. Dissolve the gelatine with the 4 tablespoons of water – then stir into the mixture.

Put the bowl into the fridge and allow to thicken, but not to set.

Whisk the egg whites until stiff, and lightly whip the cream. Fold both into the mixture. Pour into the tin on the base. Leave to set in the fridge (usually 2 plus hours).

To turn out remove the side of the tin then ease from the base with a cake slice – very carefully.

Note – the fruits can be substituted – 1 grapefruit or 1-2 oranges. Mixed fruit and/or sultanas are a good addition as well if you wish.

MICHAEL BODDINGTON, EPSOM GROUP, SOUTH EAST REGION

From Lady Angela Whiteley

Blackcurrant Ice Cream

(Serves 4 people)

½ pt (275ml) double cream OR
¼ pt (150ml) double cream AND
¼ pt (150ml) Greek yoghurt
⅓ bottle Ribena

Whip the cream lightly, add the yoghurt if you're using it. Stir in about ⅓ of the bottle of Ribena. Put into the freezer for a couple of hours.

Remove to the fridge for about an hour before using, then spoon into glass bowls or petit pot de creme.

This is very good with raspberries and redcurrants.

LADY ANGELA WHITELEY

Honorary Life Vice-President RDA. Involved in the work of RDA since 1969 when she helped to set up the Royal Mews Group in London and later the London Region. Involved in starting and organising the Ascot Race Day which helps to provide funds for RDA.

Yorkshire Curd Cheese Tart

(Serves 6 - 8 people)

6oz (175g)	short crust pastry
For the filling	
4oz (110g)	butter
4oz (110g)	caster sugar
2	eggs
8oz (225g)	curd or cottage cheese
3oz (75g)	sultanas
1oz (25g)	self raising flour.

Pre-heat oven to 375°F, 190°C, Gas 5

Line an 8" (20cm) sandwich tin with the pastry.

To make the filling cream the butter, add the sugar and beat well. Work in the eggs, curd and sultanas. Fold in the flour. Turn into the pastry case and bake for 20-25 minutes until firm and golden.

Best eaten while just warm.

Note – the fruit may be substituted with currants, candied peel, 1oz (25g) of ground almonds instead of the flour, and a tablespoon of rum, all mouth-watering.

JO WILCOX, ANGELA GERAGHTY, MARGARET TAYLOR
WELLBURN HALL SCHOOL GROUP, HUMBERSIDE AND SOUTH YORKS REGION

The group formed in 1972 and is on the southern edge of the North Yorkshire Moors. One session a week is for riding, one for driving and two or three are devoted to hippotherapy. The children have various disabilites and all the sessions are at the school. The group owns two ponies and others are kindly brought in by local owners.

Honey and Lavender Ice-Cream

This is definitely a bit different.

(Serves 6 – 8 people)

4	**egg yolks**
1 oz (25g)	**caster sugar**
1pt (570ml)	**milk**
1 drop	**vanilla essence**
2 tblsp	**fresh or dried lavender flowers or leaves**
2 tblsp	**boiling water**
3 tblsp	**runny honey**
1 pt (570ml)	**double cream**

Beat the egg yolks and sugar together. Heat the milk until it is nearly boiling, pour it into the egg mixture, stirring continuously. Return the custard mixture to the pan, add the vanilla and heat gently until just thickening and coating the back of the spoon. Leave to cool.

Make an infusion of the lavender in 2 tablespoons of boiling water. Allow to infuse for 15 minutes. Then strain into a small bowl with the honey, mix and add to the cooled custard.

Lightly whip the cream and fold into the custard mixture. Spoon into a 3 pt (2ltr) lightly oiled pudding mould and freeze for about 6 hours, stirring occasionally to prevent large ice crystals forming.

To turn out, dip the mould into hot water for 10 seconds and turn onto a flat plate.

MOY GROUP, NORTHERN IRELAND REGION

Founded in 1977 the group ride once a week, weather permitting, as they do not have use of an indoor arena. The riders are both adults and children from the local community.

Meringue Bombe Sofia

A delicious ice cream pudding.

(Serves 4 – 6 people)

For the coffee meringue

2	egg whites
1 level tsp	instant coffee powder
4oz (110g)	caster sugar
to complete	
3oz (75g)	seedless raisins
2floz (55ml)	cream sherry
6floz (150ml)	tin evaporated milk (chill 24 hrs in fridge)
2oz (50g)	walnuts
1/2 pt (275ml)	double cream

Pre-heat oven to 220°F, 120°C, Gas 1/4

The meringues can be made well ahead of time and kept in an airtight container until you make the pudding.

Whisk the egg whites until stiff, add the coffee powder and 3 tablespoons of sugar, whisk again. Lightly fold in the rest of the sugar.

Using 2 dessertspoons or a piping bag, shape the meringue mixture into rounds onto baking trays lined with parchment paper, sprinkle with a little extra caster sugar and bake for 2 hours or more until well dried. Allow to cool completely before storing or using.

To complete the bombe put the raisins and sherry into a small pan and heat gently to plump the raisins. Chop the walnuts and add to the raisins. Leave to cool.

Whisk the evaporated milk in a bowl until it holds its shape, then add the cream and continue to whisk until stiff. Fold in the raisins and walnuts.

Cut each meringue roughly into 4 and fold into the cream. Spoon the mixture into a 2pt (1 ltr) lightly oiled, pudding mould, and freeze for at least 6 hours.

To serve dip the mould into hot water for 10 seconds to loosen the sides. Turn out onto a flat serving dish. Allow the pudding at least 1 hour in the fridge before serving, to soften it slightly and make it easier to cut.

Quick tip: use white meringues and add coffee powder to the cream.

GOGARTH TUESDAY GROUP, NORTH WALES REGION

Christmas Pudding Ice Cream

This is a very rich dessert, so the portions can be small.

(Serves at least 8 people)

5	egg yolks
3oz (75g)	caster sugar
1/2 pt (275ml)	whipping cream (or double)
6oz (175g)	glace cherries
6oz (175g)	white sultanas
4oz (110g)	raisins
1oz (25g)	angelica
2oz (50g)	glace ginger
2oz (50g)	candied peel
1 tsp	all spice
2 tblsp	rum or brandy - optional
5	egg whites
2oz (50g)	caster sugar
1/4 pt (150ml)	yoghurt
6oz (175g)	fromage fraiche
6oz (175g)	toasted flaked almonds

Thicken the cream with the yolks and sugar in a double saucepan, stirring all the time to make a custard, "being very careful not to make expensive scrambled egg!" Remove from the heat.

Chop the glace cherries, ginger, candied peel and angelica. Mix all the fruit together with the all spice and rum/brandy. Whisk the egg whites until stiff, gradually adding the caster sugar.

Fold in the custard, yoghurt and fromage fraiche and finally fold in the fruit mixture (don't worry if the fruit sinks), and the toasted flaked almonds. Spoon into a lightly oiled 2 pt (1ltr) pudding mould, cover, place in freezer for approximately 3-4 hours. Remove and stir again to help incorporate the fruits return to freezer and use when frozen.

To serve – dip bowl in hot water for 10 seconds turn onto a serving dish and decorate with piped cream and glace fruits.

COBBES MEADOW GROUP, SOUTH EAST REGION

Fat Free Christmas Pudding

People who cannot take fat have a tough time at Christmas. Janet Abbot devised this recipe for her mother and now the whole family demands the same.

(Serves 4 – 6 people)

8oz (225g)	**fresh brown breadcrumbs**
4oz (110g)	**ground almonds**
12oz (350g)	**mixed dried fruit**
1 small can	**crushed pineapple in own juice**
2oz (50g)	**chopped blanched almonds**
2 heaped tblsp syrup	
2 tblsp	**brandy**
1	**white of egg (stiffly beaten)**
2 more tblsp	**brandy**
1 ct	**natural low fat yoghurt.**

Pre-heat oven to 325°F, 170°C, Gas 3

Mix together very thoroughly the breadcrumbs, ground almonds, mixed dried fruit, crushed pineapple, chopped almonds, syrup and brandy, fold in the stiffly beaten egg white. Turn it all into a 2pt (1ltr) well greased pudding basin. Cover with a circle of greased parchment paper, and a larger piece of tin foil to cover the basin, fold or tie down. Place in a bain-marie (roasting tin with about 2" of water) and bake in oven for about 1 hour.

Remove from oven, turn out onto dish, and pour two more tablespoons of brandy over the pudding. Flame if you wish.

Serve with custard made with skimmed milk, or natural low fat yoghurt.

MRS JANET ABBOTT, INSTRUCTOR, MID ESSEX MALDON GROUP, EAST REGION

Clootie Dumpling

A "cloot" is a cloth. This is a traditional pudding and may be served hot or cold and then sliced. It has sustained many a working man through a long day.

(Serves 6 – 8 people)

6oz (175g)	**flour**
6oz (175g)	**fresh brown breadcrumbs**
6oz (175g)	**suet**
1 tsp	**bicarbonate of soda**
1 tsp	**cream of tartar**
2 tsp	**cinnamon**
1 tsp	**ginger**
1 tblsp	**treacle**
1	**egg**
4oz (110g)	**currants**
6oz (175g)	**sultanas**
4oz (110g)	**soft dark brown sugar**
2 tblsp	**syrup**
1/2 pt (275ml)	**milk - approximately**

Place the cloot in boiling water. Mix all the ingredients together, adding the egg and sufficient milk to form a fairly soft consistency. Mix thoroughly. Take the cloot from the water and wring out. Lay out flat and dredge with flour. Use your hands to smooth flour out over the cloot. Place the mixture on the cloot and draw it together evenly, making sure the folds of the cloot are evenly distributed, and leaving room for expansion tie the cloot with string.

Put a plate in the bottom of a large pan and the cloot and mixture on top of that. Cover the dumpling with water. (NB if you have to add water during cooking make sure it is boiling) Simmer for 2-3 hours. Remove dumpling and place in a colander in the sink. Untie the string and gently pull corners of the cloot apart – taking care not to break the "skin". Put a plate over the colander, whip it over and carefully peel the cloot away. Serve with a suitable sauce.

Note – the proportion of flour and breadcrumbs can be varied as desired. Oatmeal is sometimes used instead of breadcrumbs. Ale may be used instead of milk.

LEWIS AND HARRIS GROUP, GRAMPIAN AND HIGHLAND REGION

Lime and Gin Mousse

(Serves 6 – 8 people)

4	egg yolks
4oz (110g)	caster sugar
1 tsp	zest of lime
1/2 oz (10g)	gelatine
2 1/2 floz (60ml)	lime juice
1 tblsp	gin
4	egg whites
1 tblsp	caster sugar (extra)
1 pt (570ml)	double cream

Beat the egg yolks and sugar until thick and creamy. Add the zest of lime. Meanwhile dissolve the gelatine in the lime juice and gin by heating gently. Add to the egg mixture.

Whisk the cream until soft, (the same consistency as the egg mixture). Whisk the egg whites until stiff gradually adding the extra tablespoon of caster sugar. Fold the cream and egg whites lightly into the egg yolk mixture. Spoon into 6-8 individual bowls or an 8" (20cm) souffle dish. Chill for 2-4 hours before serving.

PAULINE MATHER, ROMSEY GROUP, SOUTH REGION

Chocolate Mousse

This is quick, easy and delicious for children's parties.

(Serves 6 – 8 people)

2 tblsp	caster sugar
3 tblsp	drinking chocolate
3 tblsp	milk
1/2 oz (10g)	gelatine
2 tblsp	water
14oz (440g)	can evaporated milk (refrigerate overnight)
1	chocolate flake

Add the sugar and chocolate powder to the milk and heat gently until dissolved, allow to cool. Dissolve the gelatine in the 2 tablespoons of water, heat gently and add to the chocolate mixture.

Whip the evaporated milk until it is really thick and creamy, then add the chocolate mixture whilst still beating.

Spoon into 6 individual dishes or 1 large bowl and leave until set (2-4 hours) in the fridge. Just before serving sprinkle with crumbled chocolate flake.

J WHITEHEAD, ELVASTON CASTLE GROUP, NORTH MIDLANDS REGION

Fresh Fruit Icicle

(Serves 6 – 8 people)

1/2 oz (10g)	butter
2oz (50g)	ginger biscuits (finely crushed)
3	egg yolks
1/2 pt (275ml)	double cream
3	egg whites
4oz (110g)	caster sugar
1	lemon (zest and juice)
1	orange (zest and juice)
2oz (50g)	flaked almonds
fresh orange or lemon slices to decorate	

Butter a 2lb (1kg) loaf tin. Sprinkle the sides and base with the ginger biscuit crumbs. Whisk the egg yolks and cream. Whisk the egg whites until stiff, gradually adding the sugar until the mixture is very thick. Fold the egg white into the yolk mixture, adding the zest and juice of the orange and lemon, add the flaked almonds.

Pour the mixture into the tin and freeze until firm.

To serve turn the icicle out of the tin, decorate with slices of orange and/or lemon and allow to soften slightly before slicing.

PAULINE SUTHERLAND, WESTMORLAND GROUP, NORTH REGION

Orange Pastry

For mince pie or apple pie.

To the pastry mix add coarsely grated zest and juice of an orange.

Mix well and roll out.

MARY UNDERWOOD, UPTON ON SEVERN GROUP, WEST MERCIA

Chocolate Terrine

(Serves 6 – 8 people)

12oz (350g)	**dark chocolate**
1/2 pt (275ml)	**single cream**
2 tblsp	**brandy**
1 tblsp	**water**
2 tsp	**Nescafe**
3	**egg yolks**
1 tblsp	**gelatine**

Melt the chocolate or process in blender (makes a fearsome noise). Heat the cream to scalding point (just under boiling). Dissolve the gelatine and Nescafe in the water and brandy. Pour the hot cream and chocolate into processor and process, add the yolks one at a time and finally the gelatine mixture.

Pour into a 1lb (450g) loaf tin, lined with parchment paper. Leave to set for about 6 hours.

Turn out and cut into fairly thin slices – it is very rich.

Decorate.

MRS C G WILKINSON, COUNTY CHAIRMAN, MID-WEST REGION

Coffee Crunch Cream

A quick, easy and fattening dessert!

(Serves 4 – 6 people)

1/2 pt (275ml)	**double cream**
4 or 5	**crunchie bars**
coffee to taste	

Whip the cream. Crush the crunchie bars in the packet with a rolling pin, add the coffee and crushed crunchie bars to the cream and fold in. Spoon into individual dishes or a single dish. Chill well.

Note – this can also be frozen and served as ice cream.

HELEN MILLS, KYRE GROUP, WEST MERCIA REGION

A small group started in 1973 now caters for two sessions a week during term time, one for physically handicapped riders (with some riders coming from 40 miles away) and one for children with severe learning difficulties. The facilities are incredible with both indoor and outdoor arenas, lanes and fields in which to ride, but they are limited by a shortage of ponies and horses. The six they have are getting on in years. Every year the group try to have several rides to other venues, taking a picnic.

A traditional Dutch dessert.

(Serves 4 – 6 people)

2	**egg whites**
3oz (75g)	**caster sugar**
6 tblsp	**fruit syrup**

Place all the ingredients in a large mixing bowl. Whisk for 10 minutes (even longer by hand!) to reach a full volume.

Serve in individual glasses with shortbread biscuits (if available).

NORTH CORNWALL GROUP, SOUTH WEST REGION

The group has been running for 16 years. At first it was one ride a week in a field. The Princess Royal visited six years ago. Now they accommodate 4 rides a week for 25 riders, children and adults.

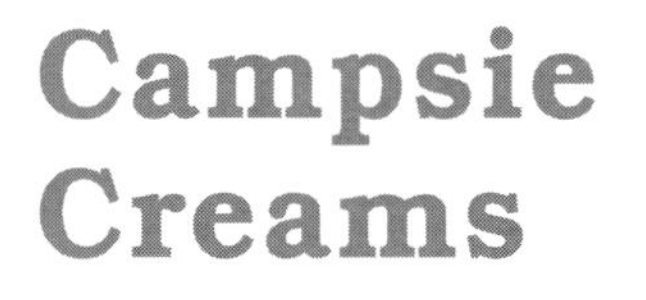

(Serves 4 – 6 people)

8oz (225g)	**crushed pineapple**
4oz (110g)	**marshmallows - roughly chopped**
1 tblsp	**lemon juice**
1/4 pt (150ml)	**double cream**
4oz (110g)	**plain dark chocolate**

Place the pineapple, marshmallow and lemon juice in a saucepan, heat gently until the marshmallows are melted, mix well. Chill, for about 2 hours.

Whisk the cream. When the marshmallow mixture is beginning to set, fold in the cream.

Spoon into individual bowls or one large bowl and decorate with grated chocolate.

FINTRY DRIVING GROUP, WEST & CENTRAL SCOTLAND REGION

Athole Brose

(Serves 6 – 8 people)

2oz (50g)	**oatmeal**
1pt (570ml)	**double cream**
4 tblsp	**clear honey**
4 tblsp	**whisky**

Toast the oatmeal till a light golden brown. Cool. Whisk the cream until thick but not solid. Fold in the oatmeal and honey. Just before serving fold in the whisky. Serve in small glasses.

BUCHAN GROUP, GRAMPIAN & HIGHLAND REGION

breads, cakes & biscuits

Guernsey Gâche

An 18th Century Recipe.

8oz (225g)	Guernsey butter
2oz (50g)	dark brown sugar
2	eggs
1lb (450g)	wholemeal flour (or plain white flour)
1/4 pt (150ml)	milk
2oz (50g)	fresh yeast
	pinch of salt
1lb (450g)	sultanas (or currants)
4oz (110g)	candied peel

Pre-heat the oven to 375°F, 190°C, Gas 5

Grease a 2lb (900g) loaf tin.

Cream the butter with the sugar, then add the beaten eggs. Mix with the flour.

Warm the milk, add the yeast and salt and leave to stand for a few minutes.

Pour the yeast/milk into the centre of the flour mixture. Mix well adding the washed fruit as you mix. Knead well, and then leave to rise for 2 hours.

Knead again and put the gâche mixture into the tin and bake for 1 hour until golden brown.

Serve sliced on its own or with butter.

Note – there are lots of slightly different recipes for Gâche but this is one of the most popular.

GUERNSEY GROUP, SOUTH REGION

The Grant Loaf

2lbs (1kg 350g) stone ground brown flour	
1 tsp	sea salt
2 tblsp	vegetable oil
3 tblsp	brown sugar
1 tblsp	dried yeast
$1^3/_4$pt (1 ltr)	lukewarm water (or water & milk).

Pre-heat oven to 400°F, 200°C, Gas 6

Grease 4 x 1lb (450g) loaf tins.

Mix flour, salt and oil in a large bowl and warm.

Add the sugar and yeast to a little of the warm water/milk and leave for 10 minutes to froth up.

Add the yeast and the rest of the warm water to the flour and mix thoroughly by hand until slippery (add more liquid if necessary).

Divide into the 4 tins and leave in a warm place to rise for about 20 minutes.

Bake for 35-40 minutes. Turn out at once and leave to cool on a wire rack.

The loaves should sound hollow when tapped.

ANDOVER GROUP, SOUTH REGION

The group was formed by Mrs A W Murdoch in 1972 and over the years has expanded into 12 sections who ride in various villages throughout the Test Valley. Both children and adults have the opportunity to ride and drive. They rely heavily on volunteers who loan and transport ponies, act as helpers and undertake administration, fund raising and organisational tasks involved in running a local group.

Bara Brith
(speckled bread)

3/4 pt (425ml)	strained tea
12oz (350g)	mixed dried fruit
1lb (450g)	self raising flour
1 tsp	mixed spice
8oz (225g)	soft dark brown sugar
1	egg, beaten

Put the tea and fruit into a bowl, stir well and leave to soak overnight, or for at least 3 hours.

Pre-heat oven to 350°F, 180°C, Gas 4, then grease and line a 2-3lb loaf tin (900g-1.35kg). Then mix the flour with the spice and sugar and add the fruit with the tea, and the beaten egg. Mix well.

Spoon into the prepared tin and bake for 1 1/2 to 1 3/4 hours. Turn out onto a wire rack to cool.

Serve thinly sliced and spread with butter.

PANTY-Y-SAIS GROUP, SOUTH WALES REGION

The group has been running for 13 years and meets once a week for two rides – all adults. They are very fortunate in having the use of a good indoor school and an arena. The riders take part in local dressage and fun days and have a good time.

Scotch Pancakes

1lb (450g)	plain flour
1 tsp	bicarbonate of soda
1 tsp	cream of tartar
8oz (225g)	caster sugar
1 tsp	syrup
1/2 oz (10g)	lard
2	eggs
a little milk to blend	

Sieve the flour and raising agents into a large bowl. Mix in the sugar and make a well in the centre. Add in the eggs and a little milk, stir well, to make a thick creamy butter. Allow to stand for 1 hour.

Melt the lard and syrup and add to the mixture, stir in well.

Grease a hot girdle (or use a heavy based frying pan) and drop on the mixture in small rounds. When the surface rises in bubbles, turn the scones over and brown on the other side.

Cool on a clean tea towel.

CATS EYE GROUP, NORTHERN IRELAND REGION

The Cats Eye Riding Group was formed in May 1993, and has four riders who come from the Cats Eye Club for blind and visually impaired people. The members who used to go riding only a few times a year now have instruction once a week, and have improved tremendously.

Potato Bread

1lb (450g)	mashed potato
4oz (110g)	flour
1/2 tsp	salt

Sprinkle the salt over the mashed potatoes. Knead in enough flour to make a dryish dough.

Roll out to 1/4 " (1cm) thick.

Heat and flour a girdle or heavy pan and place 4 inch square (10cm) pieces on hot pan turning once until brown.

THE RIDERS, LISBURN GROUP, NORTHERN IRELAND

This recipe is made by the children at the special school in Lisburn who bring the helpers little presents that they have made from time to time.

Weetabix Bread

A wonderfully sticky bread.

8oz (225g)	self raising flour
4oz (110g)	caster sugar
6oz (175g)	mixed fruit
2	weetabix, crushed
1/2 pt (275g)	milk
1/2 tsp	mixed spice

Pre-heat oven to 400°F, 200°C, Gas 6

Grease a 1lb (450g) loaf tin.

Mix all the ingredients and bake for 30 minutes. (If it is in the hot oven of an Aga, it needs only 20-25 minutes).

Turn out on to a wire rack and leave to cool.

Serve sliced with butter.

MRS M CUSHEN, TRELLACH GROUP, SOUTH WALES REGION

A small dedicated group which was formed in 1976. They cater for children from two special schools in Chepstow, in all there are 18 children who ride each week.

Sussex Sausage Rolls

(or Hikers Lunch)

"This is a very old recipe. It is recommended that they are eaten in the open air anywhere in Sussex preferably on the downs. Very good indeed."

1 1/4lb (560g)	bread dough
1lb (450g)	sausages or sausage meat

Pre-heat oven to 425°F, 220°C, Gas 7

Cut off pieces of dough and wrap them around each skinned sausage or the equivalent sausage meat. The dough should be 1/4 – 1/2 inch (about 1cm) thick. Leave to rise on a greased tin in a warm place for 20 minutes or until well risen. Bake for 15 minutes and then reduce the temperature to 350°F, 180°C, Gas 4 and cook for a further 20 minutes.

GOODWOOD DRIVING GROUP, SOUTH REGION

Cheese Scones

8oz (225g)	self raising flour
2oz (50g)	margarine
pinch	salt
3oz (75g)	grated cheese
1	egg
a little	milk to mix

Pre-heat oven to 400°F, 200°C, Gas 6

Rub the fat into the flour, add the cheese and salt.

Make a well and mix in the egg to make a soft dough. Add a little milk if needed.

Roll out to about 1/4 inch (1/2 – 1cm) thick, cut into rounds and place on a greased and floured tin. Bake for 15 minutes.

BROCKHOLES 62 GROUP, HUMBERSIDE & SOUTH YORKSHIRE REGION

Isobel's Cheese & Sesame Scones

Makes 12-15 scones

6oz (175g)	plain flour
4oz (110g)	wholemeal flour
2 tsp	baking powder
1 tsp	celery seasoning
2 tblsp	sesame seeds
3oz (75g)	butter or margarine
2oz (50g)	grated cheddar cheese
6oz (175g)	natural yoghurt
milk to glaze	
To finish	
2oz (50g)	cheddar cheese, grated &mixed with
1 tsp	sesame seeds

Pre-heat oven to 375°F, 190°C, Gas 5

Mix the flours, baking powder, sesame seeds and celery seasoning together, then rub in the butter or margarine. Add the cheese and yoghurt and mix to give a dough.

Roll out on a floured board to a thickness of 1 inch (2 1/2cm) and cut approximately 10 scones, re-rolling as necessary.

Place on a greased baking sheet and brush liberally with milk, pile some of the cheese and sesame seed mixture on each scone and bake for 18-20 minutes or until well risen and golden brown.

COQUET GROUP, NORTH REGION

Date and Cinnamon Scones

Very popular with coffee as well as tea, and of course excellent at fund raising events.

8oz (225g)	plain flour
2 tsp	baking powder
1/2 tsp	salt
1/4 tsp	ground cinnamon
1oz (25g)	margarine
1oz (25g)	sugar
2oz (50g)	chopped dates
1 tsp	treacle
	milk to mix (soured or buttermilk gives a lighter scone)

Pre-heat oven to 475°F, 240°C, Gas 8

Sieve flour, baking powder, salt and cinnamon together. Cut and rub in the margarine. Add the sugar and the chopped dates.

Combine the treacle with some of the milk and use to mix all together to a soft dough. Roll out and cut into scones. Brush with milk or egg and bake for 15 minutes.

JOYCE PARKER, STRATFORD ON AVON GROUP, WEST MERCIA REGION

Joyce has been helping with the RDA for 3 years and finds it most rewarding and enjoyable.

Grasmere Gingerbread

8oz (225g)	plain flour
1/2 tsp	bicarbonate of soda
1/2 tsp	cream of tartar
1 tsp	ground ginger
4oz (110g)	butter
4oz (110g)	soft brown sugar
1oz (25g)	sultanas (more if wished)
1 dsp	syrup
1 tsp	caster sugar.

Pre-heat the oven to 350°F, 180°C, Gas 4

Sieve the flour, bicarbonate of soda, cream of tartar and ground ginger into a bowl. Rub in the butter 'till it is like breadcrumbs. Mix in the brown sugar, sultanas and warmed syrup.

Press into a 7" (17 1/2 cm) sandwich tin, greased and lined and sprinkle with caster sugar.

Bake for 30-40 minutes until golden brown.

Cool in the tin for 10 minutes and then cut into wedges.

EDEN GROUP, NORTH REGION

Fool Proof Chocolate Cake

This recipe is used by most of our group.

For the cake	
7oz (200g)	self raising flour
8oz (225g)	caster sugar
1/2 tsp	salt
2 tblsp	cocoa
1 tsp	vanilla essence
2	eggs, beaten
5 tblsp	evaporated milk AND
5 tblsp	water OR
10 tblsp	milk
4oz (110g)	margarine
For the icing	
4oz (110g)	icing sugar
1 1/2 oz (40g)	margarine
1/2 tsp	vanilla essence
2 dsp	hot milk
2 tblsp	cocoa

Pre-heat oven to 350°F, 180°C, Gas 4

For the cake, sieve together the flour, sugar, salt and cocoa.

Rub in the margarine until the mixture resembles breadcrumbs.

Stir in 2 beaten eggs mixed with the evaporated milk and water, or the ordinary milk and vanilla essence (very runny).

Pour the mixture into 2 greased 7" (17.5cm) sandwich tins and bake for 35 minutes.

Turn onto wire racks and allow to cool.

To make the icing, melt together the margarine and cocoa, stir in the sifted icing sugar, then the hot milk and vanilla essence. Beat until thick.

Sandwich the cakes and ice.

HARTFIELD GROUP, SOUTH EAST REGION

Rich Chocolate Cake

"This recipe was first cooked by our then Chairman for tea at our RDA AGM some 12 years ago. It was so delicious that it has become the tradition that whoever is Chairman makes this cake for our AGM!"

For the cake	
8oz (225g)	plain flour
2 tsp	baking powder
1/2 tsp	bicarbonate of soda
1/2 tsp	salt
2oz (50g)	plain chocolate
8floz (220ml)	milk
5oz (150g)	butter or soft margarine
10oz (275g)	dark soft brown sugar
3	eggs
1 tblsp	black treacle
1 tsp	vanilla essence
For the icing	
1lb (450g)	granulated sugar
1/4 pt (150ml)	milk
4oz (110g)	butter
1 tblsp	golden syrup
1 tblsp	cocoa
2oz (50g)	plain chocolate

Pre-heat oven to 350°F, 180°C, Gas 4

To make the cake, sift together the flour, baking powder, bicarbonate of soda and salt. Melt the chocolate with the milk in a small saucepan over low heat, stirring occasionally. When chocolate has melted remove the pan from the heat and allow to cool. Cream the butter and sugar until fluffy. Beat the eggs in one at a time, adding a little of the flour mixture. Stir in the treacle and vanilla essence and fold in the remaining flour. Mix well and gradually stir in the cooled chocolate and milk to make a thick batter.

Divide the mixture between 3 greased 7" (17.5cm) sandwich tins and bake for 30-35 minutes.

To make the icing, put the sugar, milk, butter, syrup, cocoa and plain chocolate into a large heavy based pan. Heat gently, stirring until the sugar has dissolved, then bring to the boil and cook to soft ball stage (if you are using a sugar thermometer 240°F, 100°C). Leave to cool for 10 minutes, then beat until thick enough to spread.

Sandwich layers of cake together and spread the rest on the cake.

VIVIEN BUTLER, SEECHAM GROUP, WEST MERCIA REGION

Sticky Wholemeal Chocolate Cake

4oz (110g)	caster sugar
4oz (110g)	margarine
2	eggs
4oz (110g)	self raising wholemeal flour
1 tblsp	water
1 tblsp	cocoa, dissolved in 2 tblsp hot water, cooled

Pre-heat oven to 350°F, 180°C, Gas 4

Prepare 2 x 7" (17.5cm) sandwich tins or 1 x 8" (20cm) tin greased and the base lined with baking parchment

Beat together the sugar and margarine. Add the cocoa mixture and stir. Add the eggs one at a time, mix in one tablespoon of the flour with the second egg. Beat in the flour, adding the tablespoon of water if the mixture seems dry. Spoon the mixture into the tin(s). Bake for about 20 minutes until the centre springs back at the fingertip test.

Use a filling of your choice or eat as it is.

This recipe is also good in bun cases for picnics.

FELICITY SMETTON, OXFORD GROUP, SOUTH REGION

Banoffee Cake

For the base	
4oz (110g)	digestive biscuits, crushed
2oz (50g)	margarine, melted
For the top	
1	banana thinly sliced
1 large tin	condensed milk
1/4 pt (150ml)	double cream

Boil the condensed milk, in the tin for 1 1/2 hours

For the base mix the crushed digestive biscuits and the melted margarine together and press firmly into a 7-8" (20cm) round, loose based cake tin.

For the top place the banana evenly on the base. Then cover with the condensed milk which will be like toffee.

When cool, decorate with cream.

CLYDESDALE GROUP, WEST & CENTRAL SCOTLAND REGION

Coffee Walnut Cake

"This is a scrummy cake always goes like a bomb!"

4oz (110g)	butter
4oz (110g)	caster sugar
2 large	eggs
2oz (50g)	chopped walnuts, put into a bag and bashed!
1 tblsp	coffee essence or strong coffee
4oz (110g)	self raising flour
pinch	of salt
1 tsp	baking powder
For the filling	
3oz (75g)	butter
6oz (175g)	icing sugar
1 tblsp	coffee essence mixed with cocoa OR coffee granules and cocoa in a dsp of hot water – allow to cool
	crushed walnuts to taste

Pre-heat oven to 325°F, 170°C, Gas 3

Cream the sugar and butter till pale and creamy. Beat in the eggs, walnuts and coffee essence. Sift in the flour with the salt and baking powder and beat until well combined. If the mixture is stiff a little milk can be added.

Divide the mixture between 2 greased and lined 7inch (17.5cm) sandwich tins and smooth the surface. Bake for 30-40 minutes until well risen and springy to touch. Turn out onto a wire rack and cool before removing the paper.

For the filling – cream the butter and beat in the icing sugar, add the coffee and cocoa mix. Then add the crushed nuts. Mix and spread on the sponges. Sandwich together.

The seven minute frosting

1	egg white
6oz (175g) caster sugar	
pinch	of salt
2 tblsp	water
pinch	cream of tartar

Put all the ingredients in a double boiler (or bowl over a saucepan of hot water) and whisk preferably with an electric whisk continuously until the mixture is thick enough to stand in peaks, for approximately 7 minutes. Use at once, as in American frosting. Cover the whole cake quickly. Decorate with walnut halves.

DOROTHY CAMPBELL, BANNOCKBURN GROUP, WEST AND CENTRAL SCOTLAND REGION

Walnut Cake

6oz (175g)	caster sugar
6oz (175g)	butter
3	eggs
6oz (175g)	walnut pieces
2½oz (60g)	plain flour
	white glace icing
a few	whole walnuts

Pre-heat oven to 350°F, 180°C, Gas 4

Grease a 7 or 8 inch (17.5cm-20cm) spring form cake tin.

Note – process lightly and add "jerkily" the walnuts and the flour.

Cream the butter and the sugar until very pale and then beat in the other ingredients. (Don't fold it as this makes the cake spongier and drier rather than soft, succulent and buttery).

Spoon the mixture into the cake tin and bake for 45 minutes to 1 hour, until the cake is firm but not browned at all.

Cool it in the tin. It freezes beautifully and benefits from being kept for at least two days before eating.

Ice and decorate with walnuts.

CARLISLE GROUP, NORTH REGION

Mincemeat Cake

This is a very light, moist fruit cake and is quite delicious.

5oz (150g)	soft margarine
5oz (150g)	light soft brown sugar
2	eggs
8oz (225g)	self raising flour OR wholemeal self raising flour
3oz (75g)	sultanas
1lb (450g)	jar mincemeat
1oz (25g)	flaked almonds (optional).

Pre-heat oven to 325°F, 170°C, Gas 3

Grease and line an 8 inch (20cm) round cake tin

Place all the ingredients, except the almonds, in a large bowl and beat well for one minute or until well blended.

Spoon into the cake tin, smooth the top and sprinkle on the almonds, if you are using them.

Bake for about 1 3/4 hours until the cake is golden. Leave to cool in the tin. It keeps well in an airtight tin.

BARBARA MARSHALL, FULBOURN GROUP, EAST REGION

Farmhouse Fruit Cake

6oz (175g)	soft margarine
6oz (175g)	caster sugar
3	eggs
10oz (275g)	mixed dried fruit
2oz (50g)	cut dried fruit
2oz (50g)	glacé cherries, halved
8oz (225g)	plain flour
1/2 tsp	baking powder
1/2 tsp	mixed spice

Pre-heat oven to 320°F, 170°C, Gas 3

Grease and flour an 8" (20cm) cake tin.

Place all the ingredients together in a mixing bowl, and mix well.

Put into the cake tin and smooth the top. Bake for 1 1/2 to 1 3/4 hours.

Leave in the tin for a few minutes and then turn out to cool on a wire tray.

COTTESBROOKE GROUP, NORTH MIDLANDS REGION

Dorset Apple Cake

8oz (225g)	self raising flour
1 tsp	salt
4oz (110g)	butter
4oz (110g)	caster sugar
1lb (450g)	peeled, cored and diced apples
1oz (25g)	mixed peel
2oz (50g)	currants
2	eggs, lightly beaten
1oz (25g)	brown sugar
	jam to fill

Pre-heat oven to 400°F, 200°C, Gas 6

Mix flour and salt, rub in the butter, add the caster sugar, apples, dried fruit and eggs.

Put the mixture in two 8" (20cm) greased sandwich tins, sprinkle with brown sugar.

Cook for 20-30 minutes until firm and golden.

Turn out and cool on a wire rack and sandwich with jam.

BOVINGTON GROUP, SOUTH WEST REGION

Crushed Pineapple and Fruit Cake

This cake lasts well if not eaten first!

4oz (110g)	butter
6oz (175g)	soft brown sugar
12oz (350g)	mixed fruit
1lb tin (450g)	crushed pineapple
4oz (110g)	glacé cherries (cut in half)
12oz (350g)	self raising flour
1 tsp	mixed spice
2	eggs, beaten

Pre-heat oven to 300°F, 150°C, Gas 2

Into a large heavy based pan put the butter, sugar, mixed fruit, the pineapple (drained of the juice) and glacé cherries.

Bring the mixture to the boil, stirring regularly. Remove from the heat and pour into a large mixing bowl, cover with a cloth and leave to cool.

Sieve together the flour and mixed spice. When the fruit mixture is cool fold in the flour and eggs alternatively.

Spoon the mixture into a greased, lined 8" (20cm) cake tin (or two small loaf tins). Cook for about 1 1/2 hours.

When the cake is quite cool, wrap in greaseproof and leave for at least 3 days before cutting.

BARBARA COLLINSON, WOODSIDE GROUP, WEST & CENTRAL SCOTLAND REGION

The group formed 15 years ago and now has 3 rides one day a week. There are 25 riders, children, teenagers and adults and 15 helpers. The group bought their own pony last year and hire others, "old friends", from the trekking centre for riding on the beach and along the forest tracks. They hold an annual summer school and gymkhana and of course various fund raising events.

From Dame Mary Glen Haig

Carrot Cake

For the cake	
5	eggs
10oz (275g)	caster sugar
1/2	lemon rind
10oz (275g)	ground almonds
9oz (250g)	carrots, peeled and grated
2oz (50g)	plain flour
1 tsp	baking powder
pinch	of salt
	liqueur glass of Kirsh (optional)
1 tblsp	apricot jam (thinned down)
For the icing	
5 1/2oz (160g)	icing sugar
1 tblsp	water
2 tblsp	lemon juice

Pre-heat oven to 425°F, 220°C, Gas 7

Beat together the egg yolks and sugar until foamy, add the lemon rind, almonds, carrots and sifted flour, mixed with the baking powder and salt. Fold in the stiffly beaten egg whites and turn into a greased and floured 8" (20cm) cake tin and bake for 50 minutes. Leave to cool.

To make the icing thoroughly mix the sugar with the lemon juice and water. Coat the cold cake with this icing after just brushing with jam. Keep until the following day, at the earliest, before serving.

DAME MARY GLEN HAIG DBE

Vice-President RDA. A participant at four successive Olympic Games, winner of two Commonwealth Games Gold Medals and one of only two British members of the International Olympic Committee. President of the British Sports Association for the Disabled, 1981-90, now Life President.

Carrot Cake
(with optional cream topping)

8oz (225g)	self raising flour
2 tsp	baking powder
3oz (75g)	light, soft brown sugar
2oz (50g)	shelled walnuts (chopped)
4oz (110g)	grated carrots
2	ripe bananas (mashed)
2	eggs
1/4 pt (150ml)	sunflower oil
Optional cream topping	
3oz (75g)	margarine
3oz (75g)	cream cheese
1/2 tsp	vanilla essence
6oz (175g)	icing sugar (sieved)

Pre-heat oven to 350°F, 180°C, Gas 4

Mix flour and baking powder in a large mixing bowl. Stir in the sugar and add the nuts, carrots and bananas. Mix lightly together.

Make a well in the centre and add eggs and oil and beat until well blended.

Spoon into a greased 8" (20cm) round cake tin and cook for about 45 minutes.

Allow to cool for a few minutes before turning out onto a wire rack.

To make the topping – mix the ingredients together in a bowl, beat well and spread on top of the cake when it is cool.

NEW HALL GROUP, EAST REGION

Cheryl's Yoghurt Cake

1 x 5oz carton	natural yoghurt
1 carton	sunflower oil
2 cartons	caster sugar
3 cartons	self raising flour
3	eggs
1	lemon, juice and rind

Pre-heat oven to 325°F, 170°C, Gas 3

Using the yoghurt carton to measure all the other ingredients, mix them together and beat well.

Pour into a greased and lined 2lb (900g) loaf tin and bake for about 1 hour 15 minutes.

Turn out to cool on a wire rack.

When cool, ice with glacé icing, flavoured with lemon juice if desired.

ARUNDEL GROUP, SOUTH EAST REGION

Grannie's Cake

Very quick, needs no cooking.

8oz (225g)	butter
3 tblsp	golden syrup
13oz (400g)	biscuits, a mixture of Rich Tea and inexpensive biscuits
2 tblsp	cocoa powder

Melt the butter and syrup in a pan. Break up the biscuits to the size of dirt gravel, and put into the pan, along with the sieved cocoa powder. Mix well and press firmly into a greased and base lined 8" (20cm) loose bottomed cake tin. Refrigerate until required (at least two hours).

To remove warm the tin slightly and turn upside down onto a place.

This cake can be used as a pudding with the addition of sultanas, cherries and a little houch.

Hand the cream separately.

MRS R H KERR, COUNTY CHAIRMAN GLOUCESTERSHIRE, MID WEST REGION

Oatmeal Cake (Muesli)

$^{3}/_{4}$pt (425ml)	water, boiling
8oz (225g)	Muesli
$^{1}/_{4}$pt (150ml)	salad oil, margarine or lard
12oz (350g)	plain flour
1 tsp	cinnamon
1 tsp	ground cloves
1 tsp	baking powder
$^{1}/_{2}$tsp	salt
8oz (225g)	brown sugar
8oz (225g)	white sugar
2	eggs
2	oranges, the zest

Pre-heat oven to 350°F, 180°C, Gas 4

Pour the boiling water over the muesli and leave it to stand for about 10 minutes.

Sift the flour, and add to the muesli mixture. Melt the margarine (if using) otherwise add all the rest of the ingredients, blend well. Spoon it all into a greased baking tin 8" x 8" (20cm x 20cm) and bake for 30-40 minutes.

MARY LOUISE ALLTY CROSBY, MEIRIONNYDD RED CROSS GROUP, NORTH WALES REGION

A small outdoor group, they have use of an outdoor school and also ride along forestry paths and hills. The riders range from mature to very young.

Krispie Krunchie Cake

A teatime – all time treat. Very popular on the cake stalls and with all age groups, especially the grannies and grandpas.

4oz (110g)	butter
4oz (110g)	good quality plain toffee
4oz (110g)	marshmallows
6oz (175g)	rice krispies

Using a heavy, at least 5 pint, (2$^{1}/2$ -3 litre) capacity saucepan, melt and mix the butter, toffee and marshmallows. Stir in the krispies and press down well into a toffee tin about 11" x 7$^{1}/2$" (27cm x 19cm).

Cut into squares when cool.

ELIZABETH MITCHELL, ROCHDALE GROUP, NORTH WEST REGION

Coconut Bakewell

For the pastry base	
9oz (250g)	plain flour
2oz (50g)	butter or margarine
2oz (50g)	white fat
2oz (50g)	caster sugar
2floz (55ml)	water (approx.)
For the filling	
4oz (110g)	raspberry jam
For the topping	
5oz (150g)	butter or margarine
4oz (110g)	caster sugar
2	egg yolks
2	egg whites
2oz (50g)	caster sugar
6oz (175g)	desiccated coconut

Pre-heat oven to 375°F, 190°C, Gas 5

Prepare 1 large tin 11 x 13½ inch (27.5cm x 33.75cm) or 2x8 inch square tins (20cm).

To make the pastry – sieve the flour into a bowl, add the diced fats and rub into the flour until the mixture resembles breadcrumbs, stir in the sugar. Add water to form a soft but not sticky dough. Turn onto a floured surface and roll out to fit the base of the tin/s. Prick the base. Bake blind for 20 minutes leave to cool. Spread raspberry jam over the base.

To make the topping – cream together the butter and sugar until fluffy, beat in the egg yolks and the coconut. Stiffly whisk the egg whites and gradually add the sugar. Fold this into the coconut mixture. Spoon the mixture on top of the jam and spread evenly. Bake for 25-30 minutes until golden brown. Cool and cut into 18 pieces.

Store in an airtight container for 3 days. Freezes well.

JOAN PRITCHARD, St ASAPH GROUP, NORTH WALES REGION

Lemon Tray Bake

"Lucy's Lemon Cake is always a great favourite when we go on our Riding Holiday, or if we have to get together at anytime."

6oz (175g)	soft margarine
8oz (225g)	self raising flour
1 1/2 tsp	baking powder
6oz (175g)	caster sugar
3	eggs
3 tblsp	milk
For the topping	
1 1/2	lemons, juice & grated rind
6oz (175g)	caster sugar

Pre-heat oven to 350°F, 180°C, Gas 4

Grease and line with parchment paper a 3" (7.5cm) deep tin, 12 x 9 inches (30 x 22.5 cm).

Put the margarine, flour, baking powder, sugar, eggs and milk together in a large bowl and beat well for about 2 minutes until well blended.

Turn the mixture into the tin and smooth the top. Bake in the oven for about 35-40 minutes until the cake has shrunk from the sides of the tin and springs back when pressed in the centre with your fingertips.

When the cake comes out of the oven, mix the juice and rind of the lemons with the caster sugar, and spoon over the hot cake. If the lemons have a lot of juice, the lemon and sugar mixture will be runny, otherwise it will be more like a sugary paste which has to be spread over the cake with the back of a spoon.

Leave to cool in the tin.

Ice as required.

MOORCROFT SCHOOL GROUP, GREATER LONDON REGION

Raspberry Squares

For the base	
$2^1/_2$oz (60g)	margarine
4oz (110g)	soft brown sugar
4oz (110g)	digestive biscuits, crushed
1 tblsp	plain flour
For the top	
1 small tin	condensed milk
8oz (225g)	desiccated coconut
few drops	almond essence
For the pink icing	
4 tblsp	icing sugar
1 tblsp	lemon juice
1 tblsp	raspberry jam, home made and sieved

Pre-heat oven to 325°F, 170°C, Gas 3

To make the base, melt the margarine and add the sugar, crushed biscuits and flour. Mix well, press into a greased 7 x 7inch (17.5cm x 17.5cm) tin and bake for 5 minutes.

Meanwhile **for the top**, mix together the condensed milk, desiccated coconut and almond essence. Spread the mixture over the base and bake for a further 15 to 20 minutes until golden brown. Do not overcook. Cool slightly.

Make the pink icing and spread over the cake.

When cold cut into squares. These look very attractive as there are three layers of different colours.

YVONNE PORTER, MID-ANTRIM GROUP, NORTHERN IRELAND REGION

Ginger Horses

This recipe has been used by the group with tremendous success at all their parties for years.

(Makes about 60 horses)

4oz (110g)	**butter**
4oz (110g)	**caster sugar**
3 tblsp	**golden syrup**
1 tblsp	**ground ginger OR**
1 tblsp	**ginger & cinnamon**
10oz (275g)	**flour**
1/2 tsp	**bicarbonate of soda.**

Pre-heat oven to 375°F, 190°C, Gas 5

You will need templates for cutting out horse shapes, a large baking sheet and 2 squares parchment paper to fit. Flour sifter, small short pointed knife, rolling pin and wire rack.

Beat together the butter and sugar, add the syrup, flour and ginger. Dissolve the bicarbonate in a little cold water, mix and work all up to a smooth dough.

Flour the rolling pin and the parchment paper. Cut off about 1/4 of the dough and roll out very thinly.

Cut out horses with the pointed knife.(It helps if you have another template to plan how many you can cut out). Mark eyes with the blunt end of a matchstick. Remove surplus bits, slide paper onto baking sheet and bake for about 7 minutes until golden brown.

They will be floppy for a few minutes while still hot so leave flat while sliding a second sheet of horses onto the tray, then cool on a wire rack until they stiffen.

The bits that are left over can be worked again, it helps if they are kept warm, and if rolled out several times add a little syrup and butter to make up for the rolling out flour.

The horses keep crisp in an airtight tin for several weeks.

Note – if you want to make them look very beautiful pipe on icing eyes, manes and tails.

Cut templates out of thickish plastic, coloured rather than transparent as they're easier to see.

BARNSTAPLE AND DISTRICT GROUP, SOUTH WEST REGION

Des Mervelles

Jersey Wonders were traditionally eaten at Easter.

1lb (450g)	self raising flour
pinch	of salt
pinch	of nutmeg
6oz (175g)	caster sugar
2 1/2 oz (60g)	margarine
2	eggs
7floz (190ml)	milk

Rub together the dry ingredients and margarine as for pastry.

Add the lightly beaten eggs to some of the milk, but keep back a little of the milk until you see how much is needed (some flours vary) and the dough should be quite stiff. Knead this ball of dough well otherwise the Wonders can break up during cooking.

Divide dough into 1oz (25g) pieces, about the size of a walnut. Mould into round balls. Then roll them out into ovals, roughly 3 inches (7 1/2 cm) long and 2 inches (5cm) wide. Make one cut down the centre of each. Gently pull one end portion through the centre split and bend backwards to give distinctive shape.

Bring a pan of lard or oil to boiling point, place one Wonder in at a time. Cook one side till golden brown, turn with a skewer, cook the other side and remove from the fat. It is better if you can cook the Wonders in a wire basket as they can easily break when being removed from the fat.

They are best eaten warm.

JERSEY GROUP, SOUTH REGION

Golden Biscuits

(Makes about 35 biscuits)

4oz (110g)	margarine
4oz (110g)	sugar
4oz (110g)	golden syrup
1 tsp	bicarbonate of soda
1 tblsp	milk
1 tsp	ginger
1 tsp	mixed spice
9oz (250g)	plain flour

Pre-heat oven to 325°F, 170°C, Gas 3

Cream the margarine and sugar. Warm the syrup and add the bicarbonate of soda, dissolved in the milk, to it.

Sift the ginger and spice with the flour and add to the mixture.

Roll into balls (slightly smaller than ping-pong balls) flatten slightly and place on an ungreased baking tin. Allow space to spread.

Cook for 30 minutes. Allow to cool on the tin for a few minutes then remove to a wire rack.

SALLY RAW, OLD PARK FARNHAM GROUP, SOUTH EAST REGION

The group was started over 20 years ago by the mother and her friends of a mentally handicapped child. Since then they have built 3 stables, acquired 3 ponies, a trailer, tack, etc. They now have 2 rides for 40 children and 25 loyal helpers. Twice a year they have a long ride with a picnic.

Eight years ago the group was asked to take two ponies to the school for mentally handicapped. This is now on a regular weekly basis. The younger children have benefitted substantially from contact with the ponies. One boy never spoke at all at the beginning, now he cannot be stopped!

Caramel Shortbread

A very popular recipe for fund raising events.

For the shortbread base	
6oz (175g)	plain flour
2oz (50g)	caster sugar
4oz (110g)	butter
For the caramel	
2oz (50g)	butter
2oz (50g)	soft brown sugar
1 large can	condensed milk

Pre-heat oven to 325°F, 170°C, Gas 3

To make the shortbread, rub the butter into the flour and sugar until at the breadcrumb stage. Press into a swiss roll tin and bake for about 30 minutes until just coloured. Cool.

Meanwhile **to make the caramel**, heat the butter and sugar in a pan and add the condensed milk. Bring to the boil and stirring continuously cook until the caramel is a creamy fudge colour. Pour over the shortbread and leave to cool.

Optional extra:- melt 4oz (110g) chocolate and pour over the top.

When cool, cut as required.

ISABEL DARBY, GADDESDEN PLACE GROUP, EAST REGION

Spicy Muesli Bars

16oz (450g)	muesli
2 tsp	cinnamon
1 tsp	nutmeg
8oz (225g)	butter
4 tblsp	honey
2	eggs, beaten
3oz (75g)	plain flour

Pre-heat oven to 300°F, 150°C, Gas 2

Mix the muesli, cinnamon and nutmeg together. Melt the butter and honey and add to the dry ingredients.

Next add the beaten eggs and fold in the flour. Press into a greased shallow baking tray and bake for about 45 minutes.

Allow to cool slightly and then cut into pieces.

HAZEL CAVE, ABERCONWY GROUP, NORTH WALES REGION

French Chew

For the base	
$1^1/_2$ oz (40g)	margarine
2oz (50g)	caster sugar
1	egg yolk
pinch	of salt
drop	of vanilla essence
3oz (75g)	self raising flour
For the topping	
1 egg white	
1oz (25g)	coconut
2oz (50g)	caster sugar
cherries or chopped nuts to decorate.	

Pre-heat oven to 325°F, 170°C, Gas 3

For the base, cream the margarine and sugar, beat in the egg yolk and vanilla essence. Fold in the flour and salt. Press the mixture into a lined 8" (20cm) shallow tin.

For the topping, beat the egg white until stiff, lightly fold in the sugar and the coconut. Spread the mixture over the base. Decorate and bake for about 30 minutes.

When cool, cut and remove from the tin.

WENDY ROUSELL, SILVERSTONE GROUP, NORTH MIDLANDS REGION

Dentist's Delight

"This recipe has been in the family for years and is very popular when served at meetings. Members of Tettenhall Group say they will buy the book to get this recipe. I hope they still go to meetings now that they can make it themselves!"

3oz (75g)	**soft brown sugar**
2oz (50g)	**butter**
1 tblsp	**golden syrup**
1/2 tsp	**ginger (optional)**
4oz (110g)	**oats**

Pre-heat oven to 400°F, 200°C, Gas 6

Butter a tin 3/4 inch (2cm) deep by 7 inch (17.5cm) square.

Soften the brown sugar, butter, golden syrup and ginger and beat well, then add the oats.

Spread evenly in the baking tin, by pressing lightly with a floured fork.

Bake for at least 30 minutes, until cooked but not too well done, slightly chewy.

Whilst still warm mark with a knife and cut through so that when cold it will be in pieces.

Keep in an airtight tin.

CHRISTINE M BIRCH, TETTENHALL GROUP, WEST MERCIA REGION

Started in 1974 the group now has 50 riders, but is limited by the shortage of helpers. It is always a very busy group with riding and money raising activities.

Chackmore Chocolate Biscuits

Much enjoyed at committee meetings!

4oz (110g)	margarine
2oz (50g)	caster sugar
1/2 tsp	vanilla essence
4oz (110g)	self raising flour
1oz (25g)	cocoa powder
pinch	salt
For the filling	
vanilla flavoured butter cream	

Pre-heat oven to 325°F, 170°C, Gas 3

Cream the margarine, sugar and essence. Sieve in the flour, cocoa and salt, and mix well (or put all the ingredients in a food processor).

Roll into balls the size of a walnut and place on a greased baking sheet. Flatten with a fork dipped in water. Bake for about 12 minutes.

Cool and sandwich together with the filling. Dust liberally with icing sugar.

BUCKINGHAM GROUP, SOUTH REGION

Meeting once a week a small friendly group of 11 children of varying ages and abilities, 17 helpers and 5 hired willing ponies. Gymkhanas are held twice a year and parents and children enjoy the Easter and Christmas parties at the local pub. The highlight in the diary is entering the Best Float Competition in the annual parade for the Christmas Carnival.

preserves & miscellany

8 ponies	assorted sizes
8 riders	various ages
20 helpers	able to run
1 lively tape to make it all fun	

Mount 8 riders on ponies of appropriate size dressed to match the theme of the music. Train helpers with regular periods of trotting during lessons until fit – mix generously among the ponies. Practice ride slowly at first so that the mixture does not curdle, gradually adding the music and compiling the movements until the whole runs through smoothly – any lumps should be worked on until they disappear.

Take a warm arena in summer (indoors is preferable) and heat to 35°C (95°F). Invite an audience and, when all is ready, introduce the mixed ingredients. Start the music. Cooking time 10 minutes approximately. When the helpers reach a hot dropping consistency with fat running freely the pie is ready.

Can be served to a hungry audience of any size at any time.

CAROL RYCROFT, COURT MEADOW GROUP, SOUTH EAST REGION

A little something dedicated to the 15,000 voluntary helpers who give of their time and turn out in all weathers to make RDA possible.

Lemon Curd

(Makes about 2lb(900g))

3	large lemons
8oz (225g)	butter
12oz (350g)	sugar
2	eggs

Grate the lemon rind and strain the juice. Melt the butter and sugar together in a basin over hot water (or use a double saucepan) add the lemon rind and juice. Beat the eggs and strain into the bowl. Cook over hot water stirring constantly until the mixture thickens and coats the back of a wooden spoon. Pot into clean dry jars. Keep in a refrigerator when opened.

JANE DAVENPORT, SNOWBALL FARM GROUP, SOUTH REGION

Lemony Apple Jam

(Makes about 10lb ($4^1/_2$kg))

7lb (about 3kg) apples, peeled and cored weight	
4	**lemons, juice**
$5^1/_4$ lb ($2^1/_2$kg)	**sugar, preserving and a little lump**
4oz (110g)	**almonds, blanched and split**
1oz (25g)	**butter**

Rub the zest of the lemons on to the lumps of sugar. Grease around the preserving pan with the butter, this stops the apples from sticking.

Put the apples, cut into fairly large pieces into the pan, together with the lemon juice. Cook gently over a low heat until soft. Add the sugars, dissolve gently and then bring to the boil. Stir in the almonds. Cook for 25-30 minutes. Test for setting and pot.

HANFORD GROUP, SOUTH WEST REGION

Cheesy Olives

To be served hot or cold with aperitifs.

8oz (225g)	**flour**
4oz (110g)	**margarine**
4oz (110g)	**cheese, grated**
salt and freshly ground black pepper,	
pinch of	**dry mustard**
crunchy peanut butter, optional	
6oz (175g)	**green stuffed olives**

Pre-heat oven to 425°F, 220°C, Gas 7

Rub the margarine and cheese into the flour with the seasonings, knead the pastry and then roll out.

Carefully spread a thin layer of crunchy peanut butter over the pastry. This can be a messy job and the pastry can tear, but it is worth persevering in order to get the added nutty taste.

Wrap a small piece of pastry around each olive, ensuring that it is completely enclosed.

Place on a baking tray and bake for 10-15 minutes or until pale brown.

Note – these can be a bit fiddly and messy to make but its worth doing a large batch and freezing them.

MRS ANNA POWER, GREAT AYTON & DISTRICT GROUP,
YORKS AND CLEVELAND REGION

Oxford Marmalade

A truly superior marmalade! This recipe is not as time consuming as it looks and is well worth the effort.

Makes almost 7lb (3kg)

2lb	**Seville oranges, well scrubbed**
1	**lemon**
4pts	**water**
4lb	**granulated or preserving sugar**

Line the sieve with a square of muslin and set over a bowl. Halve the fruits, squeeze for the juice, strain into a preserving pan. Scoop out the pips and pith into the muslin, tie up the corners and put it into a pan with the juice.

Cut the orange and lemon peel into short thick strips (depending how chunky you like your marmalade) and add them to the pan with the water. Bring to the boil, reduce the heat and simmer gently until the peel is very tender and the liquid is well reduced, usually at least 2 hours. (Alternatively you can cook it in the pressure cooker).

Lift the muslin bag out of the liquid and squeeze as much as possible of the pectin rich juice into the pan. Add the sugar and stir over the low heat until the sugar has dissolved. Simmer slowly for about $1^1/_2$ hours until it is dark in colour and has reached setting point.

Remove from the heat, skim and allow to stand for about 30 minutes. Stir thoroughly and put into spotlessly clean, hot jars. Cover with waxed discs and seal while still hot. Label when cold.

FELICITY SMETTEM, OXFORD GROUP INSTRUCTOR, SOUTH REGION

Blackberry and Plum Jam

8oz (225g)	blackberries
1½ lb (700g)	plums, Victoria are the best
2lb (900g)	granulated sugar
1 tblsp	lemon juice
½ oz (10g)	butter

"This recipe is a substantial fund raiser using plums from my orchard and blackberries picked whilst out dog walking."

Wash the blackberries and place in a preserving pan. Wash, stone and roughly chop the plums and put in the pan. Simmer gently until soft, approximately 15 minutes. Then add the sugar and lemon juice and continue to simmer stirring frequently until the sugar is dissolved. Stir in the butter and boil until setting point is reached, approximately 15 minutes. Then leave the jam to cool and settle before potting.

IRENE HOLMES, ARUNDEL GROUP, SOUTH EAST

The group formed in 1979 meet every week during term time. They have 9 children and 4 adult riders, all physically handicapped. They own one horse and other horses and ponies are lent by the local riding centre. Over the years the group riders have had a degree of success in dressage, and have had qualifiers at the National Championships. One rider competed in the World Championships in Sweden in 1987 and came home with a gold medal.

Mincemeat

An excellent Victorian recipe.

Makes about 8lb (3½ kg)

2lb (900g)	apples, peeled and cored
2lb (900g)	sugar
1lb (450g)	suet
1¼ lb (560g)	currants
1¼ lb (560g)	sultanas
1lb (450g)	raisins
½ lb (225g)	mixed peel
1	orange, rind and juice
1	lemon, rind and juice
a little	nutmeg
a little	allspice
a wineglass	rum

Put all the fruit and peel through a coarse cut mince and mix all the ingredients together. Improves and matures with time.

DAN COOPER, WOOKEY HOLE AND WELLS GROUP, SOUTH WEST REGION

Wild Berry Marmalade

or hedgerow jam

"The flavour is out of this world. It has a crumpy texture from the nuts and elderberries and is especially good on wheaten or oatmeal scones."

(Makes about 6lb or 2.75kg)

1 1/2 lb (700g)	**hips and haws mixed**
1 1/2 lb (700g)	**rowan berries**
1lb (450g)	**brambles (blackberries)**
1lb (450g)	**elderberries**
1 1/4 lb (500g)	**hazelnuts, finely chopped (if possible freshly gathered but can be omitted altogether)**
3lb (1.35kg)	**sugar**
4floz (100ml)	**water**

First stalk and clean all the berries. Simmer the rowans, hips and haws slowly in the water until soft, then sieve. Put the puree into a pan together with the brambles, elderberries, nuts and sugar. When the sugar has completely dissolved bring to the boil and allow to boil for 15-20 minutes until setting point. (To test, spoon a little of the marmalade onto a cold plate, previously chilled in the fridge. Allow to cool and then push it with your finger, if it goes crinkly it is set. If it remains liquid, boil it again for about 5 minutes, repeat until setting point is reached).

Remove from the heat, skim off any scum, and then put into clean, dry hot jars (heated in the oven for about five minutes). Seal immediately with waxed disc. Cover, tie and label.

Ann Cooper says she usually increases the quantities but that this depends on patience picking and stalking!

ANN COOPER, REGIONAL PUBLICITY OFFICER,
WEST & CENTRAL SCOTLAND REGION

Apple Chutney

"A fairly basic chutney."

3 doz	large apples
2 fresh	red chillis or dried chillis
1lb (700g)	spanish onions, cut in half and thinly slice
6 cloves	garlic, peeled and crushed with a little salt
1½ lb (700g)	sultanas
3lb (1kg 350g)	demerara sugar
4oz (110g)	mustard seeds
1 tsp	turmeric
2oz (50g)	ground ginger
1 qt (2pt/1ltr140ml)	vinegar

Peel, core and slice the apples, cut the fresh chilli into thin rings and put in a large pan together with the onions, garlic and all the rest of the ingredients.

Simmer gently for 1½ -2 hours until very soft and pulpy. Turn into a crock and leave overnight before potting.

MARY WILSON, NEWBURY GROUP, SOUTH REGION

Damson Chutney

(Makes about 10lb (5kg))

1 bucket of Damsons (about 7lb, 3 kg)	
1½ pt (845ml)	spiced vinegar
1lb (450g)	brown sugar
1 dsp	salt
6 large cloves	garlic, crushed
6	bay leaves, dried and ground
6	cloves, crushed
2 dsp	madras curry
2 tsp	Fenugreek (Trigonella)

Boil the damsons in the spiced vinegar. Then de-stone them. Boil again with the brown sugar, and the rest of the ingredients. Stir frequently. Cook until tender and well blended. Bottle in clean hot jars, seal and cover.

KYRE GROUP, WEST MERCIA REGION

Plum Chutney

(Makes about 7lb (3kg))

3lb (1kg350g)	plums
3 large	onions
1lb (450g)	cooking apples
1lb (450g)	mixed dried fruit
1lb (450g)	dark soft brown sugar
1lb (450g)	demerara sugar
10 whole	cloves
2pt (1ltr140ml)	malt vinegar
2 tsp	ground ginger
2 tsp	salt
2 tsp	ground cinnamon
2 tsp	mixed ground spice

Wash the plums, then split in half and remove the stones. Core, peel and chop the apples. Peel and chop the onions.

Place in a large preserving pan, add all the other ingredients, putting the cloves in a secure muslin bag.

Bring to the boil, stirring frequently to make sure the sugar is dissolved. Lower the heat and simmer for 2-3 hours until most of the vinegar has evaporated. Stir occasionally, more towards the end of the cooking time to prevent the mixture sticking.

Pot the chutney into hot clean jars. Seal, label when cool and allow to mellow.

MARY TWIGG, HARLOW AND DISTRICT GROUP, EAST REGION

Vodka and Gypsy's Fudge

4oz (110g)	butter
5oz (150g)	sugar
2 tblsp	syrup
1 small tin	evaporated milk
8oz (225g)	crumbled digestive biscuits
4oz (110g)	chocolate, melted

Vodka is the group's own pony and Gypsy a pony owned by a helper and used regularly by the group. Both, like fudge, are great favourites with the children!

Put the butter, sugar and syrup into a heavy bottomed pan and allow to melt slowly. Add the evaporated milk and keep stirring over the heat until the mixture becomes a darker caramel colour and a thicker consistency. Mix in the crumbled digestive biscuits. Pour into a greased shallow tin, and cool in the refrigerator. Then add the melted chocolate to the top and smooth. When cool again cut into bite size pieces.

JEAN MUSSON, COURT MEADOW GROUP, SOUTH EAST REGION

The group formed in 1977 to provide riding as a therapy for pupils with severe learning difficulties and special needs from the local school. They have three sessions a week during term time for children aged from 3-16 years. The older ones enjoy an annual summer camp at the stables when they concentrate on caring for their ponies, riding and having fun.

Tablet

2lb (900g)	granulated sugar
8floz (220ml)	milk
1oz (25g)	butter
1 dsp	syrup
1 sml tin	condensed milk
2 tsp	vanilla essence

In a heavy bottomed saucepan, put the sugar, milk, butter and syrup, melt and then boil for one minute.

Take off the heat, add the small tin of condensed milk, then boil for 15-20 minutes, stirring occasionally.

Remove from the heat again, add the vanilla essence, and beat well. When it is beginning to thicken pour into greased trays.

Cut into pieces and wrapped attractively this always sells well at fund raising events.

EDEN GROUP, NORTH REGION

Non-cook Sweets

Peppermint Creams

1lb (450g)	icing sugar
2	egg whites
1/2 tsp	lemon juice
peppermint essence, to taste	
green colouring	

Put all the ingredients into a basin and beat until smooth and stiff. A little extra lemon juice or water may be added to get the right consistency. Add colouring and essence to taste. Put onto a board covered in icing sugar and knead well. Roll flat, cut out the shapes. Leave to dry.

Coconut Ice

3 1/2 oz (100g)	potato, cooked and sieved
5oz (150g)	icing sugar
6oz (175g)	desiccated coconut
pink colouring	

Grease a tin approx. 7" x 7" (17.5cm x 17.5cm).

Mix the icing sugar into the potato and add the coconut – be sure to mix well. Spread half the mixture over the base of the tin. Add the pink colouring to the remainder of the mixture and stir well. Then spread the pink mixture over the top of the white. Chill before cutting the sweets into squares.

Peanut Crunches

3oz (75g)	Rich tea biscuits, crushed
4oz (110g)	smooth peanut butter
currants to decorate	

Put a small amount of biscuit crumbs to one side for later use. Mix the rest together with the peanut butter. Shape the mixture into small balls, roll them in the crushed biscuits and place a currant on the top.

Leave to dry for about 30 minutes.

JOHN RAYBOULD, BROOKDALE GROUP, WEST MERCIA REGION

A very good toffee recipe

1/2 lb (225g)	butter
1/2 lb (225g)	golden syrup
1lb (450g)	sugar
1 dsp	water

Put all the ingredients in a thick bottomed pan and dissolve VERY slowly.

Boil for 20 minutes.

Test in cold water and then pour into a greased square tin. Mark into pieces before the toffee is set.

MRS. M. HOULSTON, WELBURN HALL SCHOOL GROUP, HUMBERSIDE AND SOUTH YORKSHIRE REGION

Lemonade

8 large	lemons
1pt (570ml)	cold water
1 1/4 lb (560g)	sugar

Pare the lemons thinly, taking care not to have any pith. Squeeze the juice. Put all the ingredients into a container, leave overnight. Strain the next day.

MRS. CORNELL, DAUNTSEY VALE GROUP, MID WEST REGION

Elderflower Cordial

Makes 4-4 1/2 pints (2.2-2.5ltrs) concentrated juice

20	Elderflower heads
2lb (900g)	light brown sugar
2lb (900g)	white sugar
3oz (75g)	citric acid
2 1/2	lemons, sliced
3pt (1.750ml)	boiling water

Wash the Elderflowers. Put all the ingredients into a large china bowl and leave for 4-5 days stirring occasionally. Cover with a clean cloth. Strain and bottle.

It keeps well in the fridge. Drink with iced water or soda water.

SUE LARGE, BRECKNOCK GROUP, SOUTH WALES REGION

Easy Apple Wine

Makes 1 gallon (4½ltr)

6lb (2.7kg)	apples
1	lemon
2½ -3lb (1kg125g-1kg350g)	sugar
1 gallon (8pts/4-4½ ltrs)	boiling water
Wine yeast and nutrient	

Roughly chop the apples, including cores, peel and bruised bits.

Place in a bucket or other lidded container. Cover with boiling water, don't use the full gallon, reserve some for dissolving the sugar. Add the thinly cut lemon rind and the juice.

When the water cools add the wine yeast, following instructions on the packet.

Leave covered and stir daily for 5 days, preferably in a warm place so fermentation will start.

Strain the apples through a muslin bag.

Dissolve the sugar in (the reserved) boiling water and when cool add to the apple juice.

Transfer to a demi-john fitted with an air lock and leave to ferment out for about six months.

Siphon off and bottle.

WENLO GROUP, NORTH MIDLANDS REGION

Stirrup Cup

- Red wine
- Guiness
- Rum
- Lemon juice
- Sugar
- Cinnamon
- Nutmeg
- Cloves
- Chopped fruit for decoration

Quantities as you wish, it mainly consists of red wine.

Serve hot.

WINDMILL GROUP, EAST REGION

Sloe Gin

"This recipe is well tried and tested by many friends."

Pick 1 1/2 pints (1 ltr) of sloes from bushes which are heavy with fruit from mid August onwards.

Prick the sloes thoroughly with a small fork (this helps the gin and juices get together). Put the sloes into a large jar adding 3/4 lb (350g) sugar and 1 quart (2 pints) 1.150ml) of gin, plus a few pounded almonds OR a few drops of almond essence. Cover the jar tightly.

Shake the jar once a week to mix, and help the sugar dissolve.

After 3-4 months the sloe gin/liqueur is ready, just in time for Christmas. The result is a deep pink, sweet-sour refreshing taste. Potent. Don't forget to eat the berries from the bottle.

Sloe gin improves with age – don't we all!

BRENDA MAY, STELLA HANCOCK DRIVING GROUP, SOUTH EAST REGION

Fresh Herbs out of season

Pick herbs freshly. Whizz them with water in the blender until they are chopped. Then pour the liquid into an ice tray with dividers in it.

When frozen put herb ice blocks in container, label and place in freezer until needed.

When using, thaw one cube in a strainer and hey presto! Freshly chopped herbs for whatever you want.

COBBES MEADOW GROUP, SOUTH EAST REGION
Cobbes Meadow have both riding and driving groups.

The Mustard

3 tsp	table salt
12 tsp	caster sugar
12 dsp	dry mustard
3 dsp	worcester sauce
2 dsp	tarragon vinegar
6½ dsp	malt vinegar

Stir all ingredients until free of lumps.

Put in a jar with a lid placing a piece of parchment or waxed paper between the jar and the lid.

Mature for three weeks.

Will keep for months in jars.

MARY WILSON, NEWBURY GROUP, SOUTH REGION
Newbury has both a riding and driving group.

Peppery Mayonnaise Dip
(for crudities)

This is very tasty and easy on calories depending which mayonnaise/yoghurt is used.

8oz (225g)	mayonnaise OR reduced calorie mayonnaise/yoghurt OR a mix of both
2 tblsp	onion, grated
2 tsp	tarragon vinegar
2 tsp	chives, chopped
2 tsp	mild chilli sauce
1/2 tsp	curry powder (to taste)
1/2 tsp	salt (to taste)
1/4 tsp	pepper (to taste)

Mix all the ingredients together, cover and chill (for at least 1 hour).

Spoon the mixture into a bowl, place in the centre of a plate and surround with raw vegetables, cauliflower florets, carrot sticks, etc.

JEAN FORBES-HARRISS, ROSSWAY GROUP, EAST REGION

Rossway have both a riding and driving group.

Non-Oily Mayonnaise

2 tblsp	sugar
1 tblsp	dry mustard
1 tsp	flour
1	egg
8 tblsp	milk
6 tblsp	vinegar
1 tsp	butter
salt to taste	

Mix the sieved dry ingredients and add the beaten egg. Warm the milk and add to the mixture. Blend well. Return the mixture to a saucepan, and heat gently, stirring all the time until the mixture thickens. Add the heated vinegar slowly, stirring all the time. Add the butter and simmer for a further few minutes.

Allow to cool and bottle.

MRS R M NORTON, HERONS GHYLL DRIVING GROUP, SOUTH EAST REGION

Ice Bowl

You will need two bowls, say 6" and 8" in diameter (15cm and 20cm)

Half fill the large bowl with water and place the small bowl inside, weigh it down and tape it at the top so that the water is evenly distributed over the base and sides of both bowls. Slide some flowers or herbs into the water.

Freeze overnight.

15 minutes before needed remove from the freezer and place in the fridge. After this time the bowls should release from the ice. DO NOT use water to release bowls as the ice will crack.

Place the bowl on a tray. Fill with fruit salad, fresh fruit, prawns, ice cream or whatever.

HANFORD GROUP, SOUTH WEST REGION

Super Saddle Soap

1 bar	**glycerine saddle soap (must be bar type)**
1 tsp	**glycerine**
1/2 pt (275g)	**milk, full cream milk works better**

Chop the saddle soap, gently melt over water (bowl or double saucepan) or in microwave.

Add the glycerine and the same volume of milk as soap mix. Stir briskly. Cool in fridge until set. Keeps well.

SUE ADAMS, LEOMINSTER GROUP, WEST MERCIA REGION

The best fruit cake ever

And finally . . .

1	cup butter
1	cup sugar
4	large eggs
1	cup dried fruit
1 tsp	baking powder
1 tsp	baking soda
1 tsp	salt
1 cup	brown sugar
1/2	cup nuts (optional)
1 or 2	quarts whisky

Before you start, sample the whisky to check for quality. Good isn't it?

Now go ahead. Select a large mixing bowl, measuring cup, etc.

Check the whisky again, as it must be just right. To be sure to be sure the whisky is of the highest quality, pour 1 level cup into a glass and drink it as fast as you can. Repeat.

With an electric mixer, beat 1 cup of butter in a large fluffy bowl. Add 1 teaspoon of thugar and beat again.

Meanwhile make sure the whisky is of the finest quality. Cry another tup, open second quart if necessary.

Add 2 arge legs, 2 cups of fried druit and beat till high. If druit gets struck in beaters, just pry it loose with drewscriver.

Sample the whisky again, checking for tonsicisity, then sift two cups of salt or anything, it doesn't really matter.

Sample the whisky again. Sift 1/2 pint of lemon juice. Fold in chopped butter and strained nuts, add 1 baBBlespoon of brown thugar, or whatever colour you fancy, and mix well. Grease oven and turn cake pan to 350°F. Now pour the whole mess into the coven and ake.

Check the whisky and go to bed!

SUSAN BROWN, BROMHAM, ELIZABETH CURTIS CENTRE, EAST REGION

the really useful wine guide

In this Really Useful Cookbook are recipes for every occasion gathered by Chris Gow from RDA groups across the country and carefully selected and tested by her before inclusion in the collection. For many of these recipes the finishing touch will be a wine selected with equal care to match the texture and flavour of that dish.

We - the buyers in Safeway's Wine Department - are proud to have received an invitation to make that selection and are pleased to be associated with this book in support of the work of the RDA. Like the RDA we are a nationwide organisation; Safeway has stores, large and small, spread from Inverness to Penzance and is therefore a natural partner, wherever you live, to offer wine matches to go with these recipes.

With very few exceptions the wines should be available in nearly every store and the choices, although sometimes surprising are the products of careful deliberation and, of course, extensive sampling. Quality, value, excitement and adventure are the watchwords of our wine-buying team and we hope that these are the works that will spring readily to your mind too when you survey the wine shelves in your local Safeway.

So what will you find in a quick canter along the shelves? As well as wines from the traditional wine-producing countries such as France, Italy, Germany and Spain, there are good buys from the New World (New Zealand and Australia), and new discoveries from emerging wine areas, too.

Particularly exciting work has been undertaken in eastern Europe where we have worked closely with winemakers to produce some thrilling new wines which offer wonderful flavours at bargain prices. These are often exclusive to Safeway as the buyer will always try to snap up any particularly impressive wines before they go on general release.

What are the names and bottles to look out for?

Wine has become a truly international affair recently with some innovative winemakers travelling the world to produce exciting new wines. One of the leading names among these "visiting winemakers" is Hugh Ryman, an Englishman who lives in France but who has made wine in a staggering number of countries throughout Europe. At the Gyongyos Estate in Hungary, for example, he produced a zingy Sauvignon Blanc and a well-rounded Chardonnay - while in Moldova he worked with the local grape varieties, Rikatsiteli and Feteasca, and against all the odds, came up with two clean fresh wines.

As if eastern Europe were not enough, he reappears in our French section with the peachy Safeway Cotes du Luberon, a superb Sauvignon Blanc from Domaine de Malardeau in Duras and a bright Chardonnay from Domaine de la Tuilerie in the Languedoc region - a wine which comes neatly packaged in four tiny quarter bottles. In Germany, he worked with the Sankt Ursula winery to produce a dry Riesling and a vivid Rivaner/ Scheurebe mix.

Another visiting winemaker who appears in several places on Safeway's shelves is Australian Nick Butler. Working with the Hungarian A'kos

Kamocsay, he has produced a fine Pinot Gris and an oak-fermented Chardonnay. Look out too for his Private Reserve Cabernet Sauvignon from Villany in Hungary and a soft Kekfrankos whose flavours are as mouthfilling as the name of the area from which comes, Kiskunfelegyhaza! He is also responsible for the firm ripe Pinot Blanc from The Czech Republic.

Italy has not escaped the attentions of "visiting winemakers" either, with Gaetana Carron from Chile displaying her skills by producing excellent Trebbiano, Pinot Grigio and Sangiovese.

Of course, excellent wines are most often produced by wineries without the assistance of a foreign winemaker. Take Bulgaria, our Safeway buyers had been constantly frustrated that the wines they came across in Bulgaria invariably seemed to have been languishing in huge barrels for a lot longer than was good for most of them. In 1993 however, some of the more adventurous Bulgarians decided to try their hand at producing some wine by what is known as "carbonic maceration" - a means of fermenting uncrushed grapes to obtain maximum freshness and fruit flavours without lots of unwanted tannins and heaviness. The results were sensational; young, vibrant, juicy wines. Safeway jumped on them immediately and dubbed them Young Vatted Cabernet Sauvignon and Young Vatted Merlot. Judge for yourself how delicious they are - and for under £3.00 too!

Moving closer to home, our range of English and Welsh wines is second to none - whether it be Surrey Gold from England's largest winery, Denbies, or the Vintage Selection from the little village of Wickham in Hampshire, Black Country Gold from Staffordshire or Cariad from Wales, native wine has made great strides forward and deserves our support. What could be more fitting than to enjoy a glass of one of these with some of the traditional and regional British recipes in the book?

Another area which deserves enthusiastic support is organic wine. These wines not only benefit the environment but they also tend to have more concentrated flavours because the vines produce lower grape yields. As handmade wines from single estates, they often cost a few pence more, but with the cheapest (Safeway French Organic Vin de Table) at under £3.00, they are certainly worth a try.

Such is Safeway's commitment to these wines that, four years ago, we instigated a national Organic Wine Challenge with the invaluable assistance of WINE Magazine and Ryton Organic Gardens. The declared aims of the Challenge were to bring together the best from the organic wine world and to celebrate its achievements. This year, the independent judging panel awarded the top trophy to Penfolds Organic Chardonnay/ Sauvignon Blanc 1993 (£5.00 in our stores) - the first organic introduction by a major producer.

The wines which have very recently appeared on shelf reveal how important customer comment is to Safeway. Realising that many people were expressing concern over which wines on the shelves were suitable for vegetarians, the decision was taken to produce two wines, a red and a white, which could be identified quickly and easily just by looking at the front label. Thus the unambiguously labelled Vegetarian White and Vegetarian Red wines have been introduced. Both are produced without the use of isinglass (from fish bladders) or gelatine (from bones) during clarification.

Vegans must wait until the next vintage to enjoy the red because egg whites were used to clarify this year's wine, but the white is suitable for both vegetarians and vegans. This exciting duo is available in all stores and, at £3.99 for the red and £3.59 for the white, they represent excellent value.

On the subject of value, bargain-hunters should certainly be scouring our shelves each January, May and October to take advantage of three unique supermarket events.

January sales are traditional hunting grounds for amazing price reductions, and Safeway goes one further with its January Bin End Sale. This is real first-come-first-served stuff. Ever anxious to be ready to move on to the new vintage of wines when they appear in the Spring, there's a great clearing of decks of the outgoing year. The sharp-eyed may also spot the odd "forgotten" wine treasure unearthed from bond, depot and store.

As the excitement of the bin end sale starts to subside, it's time for our May Wine Fair. Stores are festooned in banners and point-of-sale, extra wine stacks appear up and down the aisles and some stores conduct tastings. Up to 50 extra wines are selected by the buyers to be added to the range for the whole of May with the aim of introducing people to the thrilling, the interesting and the unexpected. Even the smallest stores carry at least 20 additional lines to ensure that the Safeway spirit of adventure reaches every part of the UK. Bargains abound: wines at £1.99 a bottle and always a major price cut on top quality wine - Meursault at £5.99 for instance!

If the May Wine Fair mostly concentrates on wines from recent northern hemisphere vintage, our October Mini-Fair brings in wines from the six-months-later souther hemisphere vintage. So at this end of the year it's the turn of Australia, New Zealand, South Africa, Chile and Argentina.

Life is always interesting on the wine shelves. Quite apart from the January, May and October events, New Vintages brighten March and April; organic achievements feature in July; medals and awards won in the International Wine Challenge fill the shelves in September . . . and then it's Christmas.

So there you have it - a whole world of wine and events just waiting to be explored. We very much hope that you enjoy experimenting with the wine and food suggestions over these pages, but do remember that they are only suggestions. Ultimately, it's what you like that counts, so do try other combinations too. Get cracking then, and have a corking - or rather an uncorking - good time!

Elizabeth Robertson, MW
Quality and Selection Controller for Wine, Safeway

Chris Gow

Chris Gow has always been involved in the business and pleasure of food and cooking. Brought up in East Anglia she was educated at St. Felix School, Southwold, and then gained a degree in Hotel and Catering Management.

Chris worked for leading food companies in the development and presentation of foods and recipes for many years. She has travelled extensively in the U.K. and abroad and lived in South East Asia for a number of years gaining experience in many different cuisines.

As a result of her broad experience she has written articles, contributed to and appeared in TV and radio programmes on food and cooking and has also presented many cooking demonstrations.

Now living in the West Highlands Chris is a long-standing supporter/ helper of her local Group of the RDA.